BECOMING A SUCCESSFUL MANAGER

Powerful Tools for Making a Smooth Transition to Managing a Team

J. Robert Parkinson, Ph.D., and Gary Grossman

New York Chicago San Francisco Lisbon London Madrid Mexico City
Milan New Delhi San Juan Seoul Singapore Sydney Toronto

Library of Congress Cataloging-in-Publication Data

Parkinson, J. Robert (John Robert)
    Becoming a successful manager : powerful tools for making a smooth transition to managing a team / by J. Robert Parkinson and Gary Grossman — 2nd ed.
        p.   cm.
    Includes index.
    ISBN 978-0-07-174164-4 (alk. paper)
    1. Executive ability.   2. Self-management (Psychology)   3. Interpersonal relations.   4. Employee motivation.   5. Management.   I. Grossman, Jack H.
    II. Title.

HD38.2.G76   2010
658.4'09—dc22   2010009220

To Susan, my wife, to my twin sons, Jacob and Maxwell,
and to my mother, Joan Grossman
—G. G.

To Eileen, my wife and partner for four decades. It just doesn't
seem possible that so much time has passed.
—J. R. P.

5 6 7 8 9 10 11 12 13   QVS/QVS   19 18 17 16 15

ISBN 978-0-07-174164-4
MHID   0-07-174164-X

McGraw-Hill books are available at special quantity discounts to use as premiums and sales promotions or for use in corporate training programs. To contact a representative, please e-mail us at bulksales@mcgraw-hill.com.

This publication is designed to provide accurate and authoritative information in regard to the subject matter covered. It is sold with the understanding that the publisher is not engaged in rendering legal, accounting, or other professional services. If legal advice or other expert assistance is required, the services of a competent professional person should be sought.

Contents

Part III: Building on Your Foundation   135

Acknowledgments

THERE ARE A NUMBER OF people to thank for contributing to the production of this text. First, we must thank all of the managers with whom we have been associated throughout our professional careers. They provided much of the research material that made this endeavor possible. Next, we owe a great deal to our literary agent, Jacquiline Flynn, whose thoughtful and insightful guidance led us through the publishing process. In addition, we appreciate the creative contributions of Lynn Miller and Jeff Shankerman. Finally, we owe a heartfelt thanks to our editor, Judith McCarthy, for inviting us to work with her; copyeditor Katherine Hinkebein; and the rest of the publishing staff at McGraw-Hill.

Dedication to Jack H. Grossman

"You give but little when you give of your possessions. It is when you give of yourself that you truly give."

—**Kahlil Gibran,** *The Prophet*

I WANT TO THANK MY friend and colleague, Jack H. Grossman, for all he contributed to this book. He is no longer with us, but his spirit lives on, and his convictions continue to be relevant.

During many years of stimulating conversation and sharing business "war stories" about people we knew and with whom we had worked, he helped shape many of my ideas.

Those ideas—and many of his own words—are integral parts of this book.

So, thanks, Jack. I'm sure you'll approve of what we have written.

—J. R. P.

I AM GRATEFUL TO J. Robert Parkinson for suggesting we lovingly dedicate this book to my father, Jack H. Grossman, who coauthored the original edition. In serving as coauthor of this revised volume, I was reminded time and again of how the principles in this book were woven into the fabric of his being. Its contents reflect the type of life my father lived and the style of helpful influence he imparted to those fortunate enough to have had him as a teacher, advisor, parent, or some combination of the three.

Dad, you can rest peacefully knowing you have and will continue to make this world a better place . . . forever.

Love always and forever to my father, teacher, mentor, and lifelong best friend.

—Gary Grossman

A Note from the Authors

THE PURPOSE OF THIS BOOK is to help you, as a new manager, quickly assimilate some of the basic knowledge you must have and actions you must put into practice in order to succeed. For you to gain maximum benefit from the material, we recommend that you keep a manager's journal. In it, note the thoughts, ideas, and insights you generate while reading. A manager's journal is also an excellent place to record your completed exercises, which are presented throughout these chapters, as well as other useful reminders and information that will help you become the outstanding manager you have the potential to be.

PART I

Knowing the Territory

Congratulations on being promoted to manager! By accepting this promotion, you assumed three essential and overlapping responsibilities: to become a professional manager, to get people of diverse global and technological backgrounds and skills to fulfill their individual and departmental objectives, and to create a spirit of professionalism and teamwork within your department, wherever they may be located.

We'll begin by taking a bird's-eye view of what your job actually is—that is, your implied promises and obligations to your staff.

As you study Part I, keep in mind three key principles you need to follow to be a successful professional manager:

- Strive to create a departmental culture that enables people under your influence to be productive and to grow, wherever they are located.
- Surround yourself with people who are trustworthy and whom you respect, both personally and professionally.
- Establish and employ interpersonal and technological communication protocols that are effective for each member of your staff.

Professionals exhibit quiet strength to make the difficult look easy.

Small acts of human kindness done consistently characterize a mensch.

1

What Is a Professional Manager?

As YOU PROBABLY REALIZE, ACHIEVING the objectives of a successful manager is an arduous job. Managing a department effectively is an ongoing process that consists of developing mutually rewarding relationships with your employees. You will need to create healthy partnerships with each of the people under your influence.

The basic ingredients of all such committed relationships are the same: mutual respect and trust spiced with genuine caring attitudes.

You'll know you've successfully created healthy manager–staff member relationships when your employees feel the department belongs to them as well as to you. That feeling, in all likelihood, will motivate them to be vital contributors to the department and will discourage them from the subtle ways in which disgruntled or dissatisfied employees can hinder departmental development. Once a genuine team spirit evolves and bonding occurs, you, your staff, and the organization for which you work will profit in every way—emotionally, intellectually, and ultimately financially.

As the manager, you need to enable the formation of such partnerships. You must preserve the integrity of each of your manager-employee relationships and protect that integrity from being threatened or invaded by negative staff members or negative workplace situations. As challenging as it may be in the diverse and decentralized workplace to create and uphold the partnerships between you and your employees, that's what you must do to succeed as a truly professional manager.

To achieve the status of professional manager, take the following actions:

- Assume responsibility for creating a fertile workplace culture—an atmosphere that stimulates people of diverse abilities, personalities, and backgrounds to be productive and to work harmoniously with one another. (You know your departmental culture is fertile when its members contribute willingly, enthusiastically, and fully toward their personal and company goals.)
- Make it safe for your staff to communicate openly and productively with you and each other, and to take intellectual risks without fear of repercussions.
- Create a structure that fosters personal and career development and growth.

- Be the inspiration and guiding force that leads your department forward.

These are tall orders, but they are, in part, the responsibilities you assumed when you donned the mantle of manager. When you accepted this position, your implied promise, assuming you want to be the best leader you can be, was to be an effective teacher, a sensitive counselor, and a master gardener. A professional and successful manager assumes all three roles.

Before we examine the nature of these roles, let's discuss what it means to be a professional manager—or, for that matter, a professional in any occupation—and what distinguishes professionals from nonprofessionals. The distinction between professionals and nonprofessionals is based on more than the results they achieve or whether or not they get paid for their work. Rather, the basic differences center on how they approach their work, how they interact with their clients or customers, and how they present themselves to the world.

Professionals Versus Nonprofessionals

Professionals know what they're doing and are in full control of their domain. This control, which stems in part from professionals' thorough knowledge of their areas of expertise, enables them to execute responsibilities with utmost confidence. Conveying a true image of quiet strength, they engender trust from the people under their influence. Conversely, nonprofessionals are unsure of themselves, in part because they lack the knowledge and experience to be surefooted. This lack of confidence in what they're doing causes them to be defensive when their decisions are questioned. Ultimately, the nonprofessionals' lack of confidence, defensive nature, and apparent lack of complete control over their domain cause others to distrust them and their judgments. Such conditions inevitably create chaos and a negative work environment.

Professionals focus their energies on fulfilling their responsibilities and achieving results, not on portraying a particular image. Because professionals believe that their actions, performance, and accomplishments speak for themselves, the positive image others have of them is based on tangible results, not on what they say about themselves. Nonprofessionals talk about what they plan to do, but their talk is generally not followed by actions. This is a symptom of their desire to create a favorable image. For nonprofessionals, looking good seems to be of greater concern than actually being good. However, in reality, they don't look good, because they don't follow through on their promises, and as a result, they are frequently criticized for "talking a better game than they play."

Professionals make what they do look easy. This is a result of their awareness of what's required to excel and their dedication to perfecting their skills. Nonprofessionals often struggle to accomplish what is required of them. It's as if they're not sure of themselves and what constitutes appropriate actions, so they muddle along in pursuit of undefined and underdeveloped objectives.

Professionals are subtle when performing their jobs. They fulfill objectives without calling attention to themselves and their activities and without flaunting their position. Recipients of their services know they're benefiting, but they don't know the minutia of what the professional is doing to effect this result. Of professional managers we have known, their staff members say things like, "I don't know what he does to gain cooperation, but we want to cooperate." Or, "I learn from my manager, but it doesn't seem that she actually teaches."

Professionals in a management position gain cooperation without domination and power without force. Not only are nonprofessionals obvious about what they do, but also their intentions are transparent and suspect. Because nonprofessionals are motivated mainly by ego rather than the desire to be of service to others, they tend to misuse their authority and power. It's as if they're wearing a shirt emblazoned "I am boss." Of course, people who work for such managers see right through them and either learn to play the manager's childish games or leave the department in disgust.

Professionals walk their talk. Their actions consistently reflect their beliefs and the principles they advocate. While some nonprofessionals may be knowledgeable and may voice sound and lofty beliefs, for the most part, their actions are inconsistent with their stated beliefs. It's as if they are two different people.

Professionals are highly disciplined and, therefore, consistently do what is required in order to move forward. They are motivated by the desire to honor their profession and to excel, and their actions are committed to these objectives. Nonprofessionals are undisciplined and tend to work only when they feel like it. In general, this is because they're not fully committed to fulfilling their stated objectives.

Professionals tend to be task and goal oriented; therefore, their efforts are appropriate and lead to meaningful results. Although they know how to have fun, and they often do, for them frivolity has its time and place. Often, nonprofessionals allow themselves to get caught up with issues tangential to main objectives. They are frequently accused of not taking seriously the jobs or projects they undertake. They are also inappropriately frivolous and allow themselves to become mired in matters that have nothing to do with attaining meaningful results.

As you can see, professionalism and success as a manager are more than merely titles, credentials, and getting paid well for what one does. They are about a person's demeanor and attitude when dealing with a disparate group of people and properly handling a variety of work-related issues or problems. The most important thing when all is said and done is, be a mensch.

Being a Mensch

Being a successful manager begins with being a good person—a mensch. A mensch is a respectful and genuine person who is sensitive and appropriately responsive to others' feelings. To qualify as a mensch, you must embody and consistently exhibit the following principles, attitudes, and behaviors in dealings with people:

- Be a perpetual student and learn from everyone, regardless of education, age, position, status, or geographic culture.
- In your desire to understand people, ask appropriate questions, in an appropriate way, at an appropriate time, and in an appropriate place.
- Act responsibly and kindly toward yourself and others.
- Listen attentively to what people say, both verbally and nonverbally, and respond appropriately to their messages.
- Demonstrate a genuine regard for all people's feelings, and accept those feelings as being valid.

- Be sensitively forthright and honest with people, leaving little to the fate of imagination and confusion.
- Don't allow defensiveness to dictate actions; all actions should be guided by a desire to be helpful and cooperative.
- Make people feel valued by asking for their opinions, requesting their help, praising commendable performance, and being polite and courteous at all times.

In short, by being considerate, righteous, and positive in all dealings with people, a mensch builds healthy communication bridges. By incorporating the qualities of a mensch into your managing style, you will foster positive communications and actions among your employees, your customers, and yourself.

In addition to being a mensch, a professional manager must fill three major roles: teacher, counselor, and gardener.

A Professional Manager's Primary Role: Be an Effective Teacher

To be an effective teacher, dedicate yourself to expanding your "students'" knowledge, skills, vistas, and problem-solving abilities. Your challenge is to provide them with all the tools and encouragement they need to become independent thinkers and productive contributors to your department. To illustrate how you might go about achieving these results, let's go back in time and identify possible role models. You may want to note your observations in your manager's journal.

Recall one or two of the best teachers you ever had. Envision them in the classroom, interacting with you and other students.

What made these interactions special? Did you look forward to coming to class, and if so, why? What specifically did they consistently do that made such a lasting impression on you?

In all likelihood, whatever impressed you about these teachers stemmed from their intent to transmit their knowledge, their desire to help you understand the material they were teaching, and their commitment to stimulating you to think clearly and independently. Chances are their genuine caring made you feel special and encouraged you to develop a strong interest in what you were learning. Finally, they probably never said or did anything to embarrass you, even when you asked a question that you, and perhaps your classmates, thought was dumb.

To be a professional manager, you should aspire to exhibit qualities similar to those exemplified by outstanding teachers, but remember: your success as a manager depends, to a significant degree, on the effectiveness of all your staff members. That is why you should do everything within your power to help your employees realize their potential. You do that by exercising your power responsibly, just as your great teachers did. Always respond appropriately to questions without making the questioner feel stupid or guilty. And when it has become clear, through tangible results, that your employees learned what you taught them, reinforce their learning with sincere praise and acknowledgment.

What else can you do to stimulate your "students'" desire and ability to learn and develop? Keep this question in mind while reading the rest of this section. At the end, write down your thoughts, ideas, and insights in your manager's journal. When it's appropriate, put these thoughts into practice, and monitor the results of your actions.

A Professional Manager's Secondary Role: Be a Sensitive Counselor

Companies often get more than they bargain for when they hire someone. While companies hire people for their abilities, intellect, skills, and potential to contribute to the organization, they will also receive each employee's unique attitudes, emotions, and interests. Because staff members are people first and producers second, their productivity is affected emotionally by experiences and events both at home and at work. This is especially relevant for remote staff members. As a professional manager, one significant challenge is to stabilize a range of emotionally charged issues and divergent perceptions that evince anger, sadness, jealousies, upsets, and more. These situations will require you to be a sensitive counselor, which is an integral part of being a professional manager.

In the role of counselor, you are an authority figure whose objective is to listen attentively and sensitively to employees who trust you. By listening thoughtfully, you demonstrate that you genuinely care, and your recommendations will be taken seriously. Realize that neither you nor anyone else can solve another person's problems; each of us must assume that responsibility ourselves. However, in acting as a concerned and sensitive counselor, invite troubled employees to talk about what is interfering with their effectiveness and then offer options for resolving difficulties. The goal is not to develop a therapeutic relationship with an employee, as would a psychologist, psychiatrist, or social worker. Rather, conduct one or two productive meetings with a troubled employee that address specific behavioral symptoms that have job-related negative consequences.

A Professional Manager's Third Role: Be a Master Gardener

If you ask serious gardeners what the secret to their success is, they'll tell you something along the lines of: "First, I have to create a fertile culture that stimulates healthy plant growth. Next, I must ensure that the different species of plants in the garden are compatible. And finally, I have to maintain the garden by watering, cultivating, weeding, and fertilizing it, and by providing special attention to plants that require it." Master gardeners will also tell you that this is a full-time job yielding great joy when they see the positive results of their efforts.

It doesn't require much of a stretch to apply the rules and principles of successful gardening to being a successful professional manager. The "human plants" you choose to be part of your departmental garden have to reflect your values and be willing to contribute to your vision of what you want your "garden" to produce. Assuming you hire capable, high-potential, and conscientious people, your abilities and skills as a manager will determine how productive and responsive they will be. The chance of managing a cooperative team that's full of potential is great if you do your job well.

A significant part of your job is to see to it that "weeds" and other threats to the health of your departmental garden don't drain it of its nutrients or adversely affect employees' morale and productivity. The single most treacherous weed with which you will need to contend is defensiveness.

Helping you fulfill each of these three roles so you can become an excellent professional manager is our aim. Make this book your personal guide for building a solid, long-lasting departmental foundation and healthy structure. By approaching this material as you would an ongoing one-on-one seminar designed just for you, you can realize the implied promise of the book's title. We wish you success in making a graceful transition from managing yourself to managing others!

Discovery Lesson

Do you know someone in your personal or professional life who exhibits quiet strength? They just get things done, with little fanfare or friction. The next time you see them, watch what they do and note a few examples that you notice. Specifically, note:

- What they accomplished

- How they make people around them feel

- What made it different from someone else trying to accomplish the same task

Questions to Consider

- *Regarding the best teachers you ever had, did you look forward to their classes, and if so, why?*

- *What specifically did they consistently do to make a lasting impression on you?*

- *What specifically can you do that would make your employees look forward to coming to work every day and approach their jobs with enthusiasm?*

- *How can you move right on the continuum between nonprofessional and professional manager?*

Sensitivity is as important to managing people as music is to dancing.

A professional manager is an effective teacher, a sensitive counselor, and a master gardener.

2

Defining Your Role

BEFORE YOUR PROMOTION, YOU MANAGED only one person: yourself. In this limited managerial function, your efforts and effectiveness alone determined your success. You must have been good at what you were doing or you wouldn't be in your current position of departmental manager. But your "doing" skills that were once admired and rewarded are not the only ones you get paid for now. The new rules for succeeding are substantially different.

In your role as departmental manager, your two main responsibilities are:

- To stimulate the members of your staff to be the best they can be

- To meld a diverse group of skilled individuals into a cohesive team of people who work well together to accomplish the goals you've been charged to achieve

Your likelihood of fulfilling those two responsibilities will increase if you embody this precept: As a manager, I am only as good as the people under my influence; therefore, helping them become as effective as they can be is my number one priority.

In your managerial position, you are like a master gardener. Of course, the garden of which you're in charge consists of people, who are considerably more complex than varied flowers and vegetation, but they both require fertile soil as well as proper care and feeding for them to fulfill their potential. Some people, just like exotic flowers, may even require special treatment. Regardless of their differences, what's obvious about both gardens is that neither can ever be taken for granted if it is to flourish.

Making Sure Your Garden Flourishes

Because you head the department, all actions and standards of performance must reflect your mission, your values, and your philosophies concerning the way people treat others both within and outside the group. Being your garden's chief architect, you must establish its culture and make sure the people under your influence perpetuate the principles that govern it.

As you embark on your first important project, which is to mold your department's culture, keep in mind a quality common to excellent managers we have known. We call that quality quiet strength.

Managers who possess quiet strength have a positive influence on others without being obvious in their methods. They are clear about what they expect and desire from the people with whom they interact. After making sure their expectations and desires are reasonable, they unobtrusively do what's necessary to achieve both their expectations and their desires.

Their subtle actions, which prompt others to respond favorably to them, reflect genuine caring attitudes that say, in effect, "You are important to me," "I value your contributions," "I respect you and your abilities," and "I trust your judgment."

If you adopt such attitudes in your dealings with your staff, you will stimulate all members to produce results of which you and they will be proud, regardless of whether they work next to you or with you from across the world.

In contrast to quiet-strength managers are those who manage by intimidation. Typically, these managers overpower people with their authority. They yell, threaten, pout, send threatening messages, or do whatever else they can to instill fear in people under their influence. Although they may get short-term results, more often than not, such misuse of authority results in defensive behaviors, which prevent employees from consistently doing their best. Particularly, in the virtual community, such resistance could be undetected until there are serious repercussions.

Assuming you want to establish quiet strength as a philosophical foundation for effectively managing your department, be sure all of your employees are aware that you plan to abide by the following three-part code of conduct.

What I Get Paid to Do

- I get paid to create a collaborative environment in which all contributors are motivated to be the best they can be.

- I get paid to help everyone understand how we can work together to achieve our department's objectives.
- I get paid to ensure that we are all clear about our roles in upholding the ideals and standards that define our department.

Frame this reminder, and make it visible in your work space for all to see. (See the Appendix for reproducible text.)

Just as fertile soil is essential for a crop to grow, a fertile departmental culture is a basic requirement for people to be productive and cooperative. This serves as a reminder of what it takes to create and sustain that culture.

Creating a Departmental Mission Statement

Your company probably has a mission statement that conveys the purpose of its business and how it intends to accomplish its objectives to all of its employees and to the world outside. Essentially, this statement is the company's constitution.

Although this document is useful, it is also beneficial to create a departmental mission statement that embodies your ideals—those you would like your employees to embrace. Whether you've inherited the department that you are managing or are responsible for forming a new department, enlist the help of your staff to develop a mission statement that reflects both your and their ideals, needs, and styles.

To be meaningful, the department's mission statement should answer the following questions:

- What's the ultimate purpose of our department?
- How will our department accomplish its objectives?
- How can our department make a difference to the people we serve?
- What would we expect to receive if we were our own customers?
- What are the standards and philosophies our department intends to live by?
- What makes our department important?
- How do we proactively adjust our purpose to successfully deliver against the changing needs and demands of the business?

After you and your employees answer these questions, use your responses to arrive at a statement that summarizes your department's reason for being and how you intend to achieve your objectives, through the combined and varied talents available.

There is no one right way of creating a departmental mission statement, since it's a personal reflection of your values, your ideals, your vision of the department's character, and how you want the department to function.

Once you have arrived at a mission statement that is viable for you and your staff, distribute a copy to each member of your staff and request that they review it often.

Consistently Leading by Example

Your staff can view your departmental mission statement as mere words, or it can be taken seriously. Since you want it to be taken seriously, your actions must conform to its dictates. It is demor-alizing to people to be managed by someone who is seen as a hypocrite—a person who talks a better game than he or she plays. How can such a person be trusted? How can such a person be respected? To be trusted and respected, you must live your mission statement and strongly encourage your staff to do the same.

The following creed, which you might also want to frame and put on your wall, can guide you in backing up your words with actions. (See the Appendix for reproducible text.) Throughout this book, we elaborate on the 11 essentials it contains.

Essentials for Managerial Excellence

Be sensitive to people's feelings, and be kind to them.

Take time to make people feel special.

Listen to people's emotions as well as words.

View people's needs and wants as valid.

Choose your battles wisely.

Respect people's differences.

Avoid being defensive and placing people on the defensive.

Give people the benefit of the doubt.

Resolve interpersonal problems as quickly as possible,
   preferably before parting for any significant time.

In short, treat people the way you would like to be treated: as
   a valued friend.

Finally, never take people for granted—never.

Can you think of other, personal essentials for managerial excellence?

Genuine caring attitudes are key requirements for creating a fertile culture. The nature of attitudes, why they're important, and how you can develop attitudes that influence others to cooperate with you are the subjects of the next chapter.

Questions to Consider

- *What am I paid to do?*

- *What is my department's mission?*

- *What do the people who work for me need from me to be most successful?*

- *What are some other essentials for managerial excellence in addition to the 11 listed?*

Treat people as if they are the most important person to you at that moment.

3

The Staff Mosaic— Working Together

VALUE RESULTS FROM BUILDING A culture and skill set in which your staff members complement each other's strengths and offset each other's weaknesses. Your challenge as a manager is in the ability to understand each member's contribution, fit, and comfort level within the group. Success occurs when the group members understand those dynamics and collaborate successfully by themselves.

The workplace today is not necessarily a physical place. And your workforce is no longer an easily identified group of people in a single location. The people may come from around the world and bring varied backgrounds, cultures, and experiences. Nevertheless, as a manager, your opportunity for success depends on your ability to take those differences into account as you lead your department or company.

The principles, stories, and Discovery Lessons in this book will help you understand and adapt to the dynamic, environmental challenges inherent in your world as a new manager. Throughout the process, you will learn to effectively evaluate and leverage the challenges and gifts of today's environment to grow your departmental garden productively and profitably.

The environmental challenges include:

- Capturing the value and mix of four generations of workers
  Managing the gift of a multigenerational workforce

- Harnessing the value of technological innovation and access to real-time information
  Managing the gift of technology as a means, not an end

- Aligning the efforts and purpose of virtual communities and global resources
  Managing the gift of multicultural and remote contributions

When managed correctly, today's combination of the generational mix, technological advances, and cultural diversity can provide you sustainability, flexibility, and departmental strength. However, your staff's individual and collective success and contributions are directly related to what you do and how you work *with* them. As you reflect on the principles and perspectives in this book, think about how to incorporate them into your goals, attitudes, and interactions as a manager.

Management has been defined as "the art of getting things done through people." In a world that is more agile and portable, that definition has changed. Management now is "the art of getting things done through *people of multiple generations, across the world, while leveraging technological innovations.*" While writing the afore-

mentioned concept took fewer than the 140-character limit in sharing an idea through common instant-message vehicles, learning
how to succeed as a manager in your new environment requires
a bit more clarification and explanation. The anecdotes, theories,
and Discovery Lessons ahead provide a framework for helping you
manage and measure your departmental community successfully.

Who Are the Workers in Today's Workforce?

Workers today come in four varieties (sounds like advertising,
doesn't it?):

- Traditionalists
- Baby Boomers
- Generation X
- Generation Y

These aren't just labels; they define individuals with different
work habits, expectations, and attitudes. Individuals from each
group bring valuable contributions. Whether the value is a unique
factor to the equation, a new piece to the puzzle, their two cents,
an essential cog in the wheel of progress, or a distinct tweet to the
discussion, it is up to you as the manager to encourage all of them
to share their skills constructively and cooperatively. By learning the motivations and generational influences of each segment,
managers can leverage the individuals' talents and capitalize on
the diversity of the teams. But it is not easy.

How do you navigate a conversation among different people
where some see technology as a simple convenience, others call it

a complication, and still others see it as an integral way of life? You must understand the people behind the conversation.

Consider the varied factors that might exist in your workforce. Traditionalists and early Baby Boomers grew up in an age of hierarchical structure, having to justify themselves, pay their dues, and bide their time. They differ from younger generations in how they interact at work and process information. They are less tech-savvy than younger generations, and they prefer in-person interaction to e-mails and technological gadgets. Therefore, the best way to engage this generation is through face-to-face interaction.

Late Baby Boomers, Gen Xers, and Gen Yers (also known as the Millennials) grew up in the more volatile global economy fraught with mass layoffs, downsizings, and off-shoring. These relatively younger groups learned from the do-more-with-less mantra. So, that's what they do.

Gen Yers, with current numbers estimated as high as 70 million, are the fastest-growing segment of today's workforce. Often they want only bits and pieces of information, specifically, the parts they feel are most important to them to accomplish their tasks. In some circumstances, these individuals may not be as comfortable with their face-to-face interpersonal communication skills. It results from their reality in which much of their social interaction has been over instant or text messaging, cell phones, and e-mail.

Overall, younger generations are used to working in a fast-paced environment and getting information instantly. However, short, abrupt communication, which may seem comfortable and efficient, may omit details and humanness that may be required to deliver adequate responses. Older generations, on the other hand, may overinform, causing confusion or extra work in sifting out pertinent information. Obviously, either of these independently can cause serious problems for a manager if they are not matched with complementary workers. One solution is to match complementary workers based on their generational skills as well as their functional skills. At the end of this chapter we provide a table of "generational traits." The Discovery Lesson will encourage you to review your staff and see how to best match people based on their relative strengths and weaknesses. Here are a few examples of how to do that.

Gen-Y folks are creative, optimistic, achievement-oriented, and tech-savvy. They seek out creative challenges, personal growth, and meaningful careers. So what do they want? They look for supervisors and mentors who embrace their creative energy and encourage their professional development.

Traditionalists can teach Gen-Y folks the value of finesse, face-to-face conversations, and building trust over time. At the same time the Traditionalists can feed off the creative energy and technological mastery Millennial or Gen-X team members possess. Then everybody wins!

Baby Boomers often equate high salaries and long hours with success and commitment to the workplace. High levels of responsibility, perks, praise, and challenges motivate members of this generation. Members of the Gen-X generation have an entrepreneurial spirit. They are independent, resourceful, and self-sufficient. Gen Xers value working alone, and having both freedom and responsibility. How do they work well together? Gen-X members might learn how to work better in a team environment, while Baby Boomers might learn some efficiencies and success through life balance.

Yes! There is a great attitudinal and behavioral divide among generations. But with awareness, understanding, and willingness the successful manager can bridge the divides and produce harmonious collaboration.

The following table highlights just a few of the personal, social, and professsional qualities that define each of the four generational groups.

The Traditionalist

Born between 1927 and 1945 — Now in mid-60s, 70s, and 80s

Many retired or working part time — Resist e-mail and technological devices

Hardworking and loyal — Team players

Worked for only one employer — Less tech-savvy

Prefer in-person contact — Comfortable with lengthy meetings

Baby Boomer

Born between 1946 and 1964 — Now in 40s, 50s, and 60s

Loyal to employer — Work-centered

Look for praise — Equate salary with long hours and hard work

Motivated by responsibility — Look for challenges

Generation X

Born between 1965 and 1980 — Now in 20s, 30s, and 40s

More than 60% attended college — Ethnically diverse

Independent, self-sufficient — Value freedom and responsibility

Technologically adept — Prefer flexible work

Motivated by challenges — Willing to change jobs

Eager to learn new things — Thrive on creative input

Generation Y

Born between 1981 and 2000 — Now in their mid- to late 20s

Achievement-oriented — Tech-savvy

Look for creative challenges — Seek out personal growth opportunities

Multitaskers	Prefer technology to face-to-face contact
Resist going to meetings	Prefer Web-based instruction
Work remotely	Stay connected 24/7
Motivated by immediate praise	Reassured by frequent validation/feedback

It's easy to see the challenge that managers face in dealing with such varied personalities when they are in the same work group.

How Do You Manage Them in a Virtual Community?

Regardless of where you are located, each individual has ever-increasing personal and professional responsibilities that pull us from collective goals and objectives. So, how do you keep your staff members—whether they are on-site or remote—interested, engaged, and invested?

We feel it is best to look at the most challenging case, virtual employees. Have you ever known anyone who is visually challenged or hearing impaired? If so you may already know that when one sense is removed, the others are heightened. Any input to the remaining senses has a greater impact. The same applies to remote employees. Therefore, when working with virtual employees who cannot see you, all interactions and communications have to be thoughtful and respectful. We recently spoke with a director at a best-in-class virtual company. She shared some of her organization's principles for success, which can be helpful for managers of any company.

Success requires a commitment or magnetism to hold the members together as they sell and deliver. We asked her, "What is the company's formula to maintain that attraction?"

She said that members of a virtual community require a clear set of goals, a mission, and a shared understanding of purpose. They also need to have freedom and flexibility to deliver on their timetable within the deadlines they have been given. "Everyone knows that as part of the company we work to avert crisis. The best way to achieve that includes establishing formalized communication, respecting standing appointments, and establishing checkpoints during a process or project."

She summarized by saying, "Everything we do is evaluated around [the question], how is this helping our customer?" So, it is not about the individuals; it is about helping the customer.

To empower the employees, they want to know:

What needs to be done
When it needs to be done
Who is responsible for getting it done
Why it needs to be done
How success will be measured

Managers are responsible for:

Clarifying what needs to be done
Encouraging flexibility concerning how it gets done
Allowing for cultural and generational differences
Incorporating the strengths of all team members
Letting goals dictate the technology used, not
    vice versa
Providing for continuous verification and validation

In another section, we'll discuss delegation in more detail, but for now, think about how it worked in this U.S. space program challenge.

Once President John F. Kennedy decreed the United States would put a man on the moon within a decade, new ideas and new approaches were developed to meet the challenges of space travel. An entirely new industry was born, and new technology was developed to achieve the president's lofty goal. If the engineers continued to use only the traditional construction techniques they would not have produced the modern spacecraft. Consider this: If the NASA engineers had used traditional techniques, they would have put wings on a locomotive in order to have a powerful machine that would fly to the moon. The locomotive is certainly a powerful machine, and everyone knows wings are necessary for flight. Putting them together would seem to be a logical solution to the challenge.

Logical, yes, but it wouldn't work. Instead, new perspectives resulted in new solutions. Such creative thinking "outside the box" allows ideas to soar and interesting results to present themselves. Take the lessons of managing a virtual community into your world and perhaps you and your staff might develop your own business version of a spacecraft rather than putting organizational wings on a corporate locomotive.

What Do They Use to Communicate?

Communication has always been about moving information from one person to another, and exchanging ideas requires a set of tools to move the data. As the tools have changed, so have the techniques and the speed of moving those ideas. When this country was founded, sending a message via mail back to England

and receiving an answer could take months. That's what people expected, and that's what they accepted.

Now, due to the increased functionality of cell phones, social networking sites, Internet chat tools, and other such vehicles, an exchange requires only minutes or seconds.

That can be good or it can be bad. Inaccurate information travels just as quickly as accurate information, so it's possible to send bad messages with blinding speed. In business, accuracy is the responsibility of the manager.

What Are the Communication Options?

As you take on the new role of being a manager, look at the communication options you have at your disposal. All messages have two components: content—what is delivered; and the packaging and delivery of that content—how it is structured and sent.

Let's look at each component. Certainly, as a manager you are the content expert. We'll concentrate on the structure and sequence of your messages because you know what needs to be accomplished.

A brief review of the communication process is in order here so that you determine *what* you do, *why* you do it, and *how* you do it to assure that all steps are deliberate rather than habitual or simply comfortable.

The most important element in the communication process is what the receiver thinks your message means. As a manager, you already know what you want and why, but the messages you send aren't for you. They're for someone else. Consider what factors will influence how the person on the receiving end will interpret what you send.

That's why the generational characteristics are so important and deserve so much attention. When you have a clear understanding of those factors, then, and only then, can you deliver a message that will be understood as you intended it to be.

Design a message that will be clear to the receiver, not just convenient for you. How can you do that? First determine the point you intend to make. The members of your staff don't need to know everything you know, but they want to know what is relevant and important to them for their success. That means before sending your messages, you must edit them. Make your point, and move on. Unless there is a good and compelling reason to do otherwise, include only the following items, and sequence them in this order:

- What you want them to do or to know
- Why it is important
- How they might do it

Once again, make your point and move on. If members of your staff need or want more, they'll ask for it.

Don't assume everyone wants everything. That can lead to excess verbiage. If you present too much data you increase the potential for confusion and inaccurate interpretation.

In constructing messages ask yourself these four questions:

1. What do I want to convey?
2. What must I do or use to do that?
3. Who is getting this information?
4. What does he or she need to accurately understand it?

The only way to answer these questions is to think about your staff members before you structure your message and select your delivery medium.

The greater the distance between you and your staff, the greater the probability for error. When you are face-to-face you have immediate and varied feedback. All the physical cues are present in real time: eye contact, gestures, posture, volume, pacing, and so on. And your entire team can be physically present. When you move into mediated communication, however, you'll experience both benefits and limitations. Here are just a few examples.

Option	*Benefits*	*Limitations*
Phone conferences	no travel or downtime immediate feedback and response	only voice sometimes time delay
Voice mail	like phone conference, but no feedback	delayed response
Web conference	no travel or downtime easy to show material	sometimes poor visual quality, time delay, "jumpy" pictures
E-mail	instant, worldwide low cost	limited to print material, subject to writing ability
Text messaging	instant	limited number of characters per message

Evaluate your options and choose what is best for your situation. It may not be the cheapest or fastest method; it's the one that gets your message heard and understood.

Verify Before Moving On

Remember to "check in" during and at the conclusion of the transmission.

Verify to be sure your message was received as you intended it to be.

Again, as distances increase and cultures interact, the possibility for error expands. Here's an amusing example of what can go wrong between sending and receiving a clear message. And this was face-to-face, so think what can happen with distance.

At a restaurant in Cologne, Germany, a guest ordered a dry martini before dinner. When the waiter returned, however, the guest was served three martinis. You can imagine the surprise.

He said "dry," but the German waiter heard *"drei"*—German for "three"!

This was funny in that setting, but such a misunderstanding in business communication can be serious.

You must also be sure your American English words don't take on different meanings as you move to other countries either in person or through technology. Years ago we were given a "translation dictionary" for English to American and American to English. We thought it was a joke until we looked at it carefully. Many words in American English have very different meanings in the United Kingdom.

Here's a clear business example: In the United States the word *table* as in "to table a discussion" means to postpone the discussion until a later time. In the United Kingdom, it means, "to open the discussion right now." Imagine the confusion at a meeting if one party was from the United States and another was from Britain, and both were arguing "to table" an item?

Oscar Wilde, the poet, once described the United States and the United Kingdom as "two countries separated by a common language." He was right, and it's a good reminder for managers in a global workplace. Keep that in mind as you communicate with your team. No matter what the medium, be sure to be specific. Say what you mean, and then verify.

You can begin by avoiding vague words. That's easy to say, but the English language is so filled with vague words we often overlook them. The resulting confusion can be costly in human and corporate capital.

Here are a few to put on the top of your vague words list because they can easily be misunderstood.

Too big	ASAP
Too small	Close
Too expensive	As soon as you can
Soon	Cost
Often	Profit
Few	Ready
Many	Done

Be aware of them and beware of causing confusion.

As a manager, you'll work with everyone on your team, but in the business world of today—and tomorrow—the members of that team might be located in Bangalore, Chicago, Paris, and Sao Paulo; and you have to be sure every party understands every other party.

As workers are added to your roster and customers are added to your book of business, learn about each one of them because all business is person-to-person. Get to know the global participants: what is important to each one, and how to be of the most service and assistance to all of them. Think individuals—not groups.

Advancements in technology have removed barriers to inter-action and information, but they often create confusion and conflict. For example, e-mails and instant messages are written quickly to share a thought, but they often leave behind the respect necessary to communicate a message completely. Managing is an ever-changing art with increasing demands and challenges. And managing requires creativity. The core barriers to working in virtual communities are neither cultural nor technological. They require the ability to ask questions and to make decisions. Those questions must be the *right* questions about what the team requires.

The responses likewise empower team members to make their decisions from their understanding of the common goals.

In a later chapter you'll find an extensive section on getting to know the members of your workforce.

As you navigate through the book focus on specific people you know and how to get the most productivity and loyalty from each one.

An effective and successful manager gets work done through other people, not through giving orders or writing memos.

Congratulations!

Discovery Lesson

Choose one of the five senses at a time and imagine it is gone. Then answer each of the following questions according to the senses you have left to determine what you need for clear communication. Also consider the implied questions that go with each of those listed. For example, "What feedback do you need from your team?"

If you cannot see them, how do you know they are happy, interested, or productive? What can you do to better understand?

continued

Discovery Lesson   *(continued)*

- What support do the members of your virtual community need from you?

- What can you do to motivate your virtual team?

- How will you know it worked?

- What feedback do you need from your team?

- What feedback do they need from you?

- How will they—and you—provide it?

    How will you leverage the strengths of all your team members?

Questions to Consider

- *What am I doing to create and maintain magnetism between the staff members and our collective mission and objectives?*

- *What technologies will work for me? Which ones won't?*

- *What is my strategy for creating the best mosaic given the mix of people, the dynamic workplace, and technology limitations?*

> *Knowledge is power. To increase your knowledge, welcome your employees' opinions, criticism, and questions.*
>
> *Managing is an ongoing process of developing mutually rewarding relationships with your employees.*

4

Understanding Each Person in Your Department

PICTURE IN YOUR MIND'S EYE the best manager you've ever had. Now answer this question: On a scale of 1 to 10 (with 1 being the lowest), how well did this manager know and understand you? You probably gave the manager you envisioned an 8, 9, or 10. The key is to remember why you felt that person earned that score.

What do managers communicate when they take the time to know and understand their employees? Speaking from our own experiences with managers and from interviews with others, these are some felt but unspoken messages:

- I care about you as a person.
- You are important to me.
- I want to know how to talk to or message you and not offend you.
- I want to know how to motivate you to be the best you can be.
- I want to know your vocational aspirations.
- I want to know what excites you, independent of vocational success.
- I want to know what's important to you and what isn't.
- I want to know what specifically you expect from me as your manager.

Because those messages made the recipients feel valued, the workers responded in kind by doing everything in their power to extend themselves for their managers. Wouldn't you, if you felt valued? With the increasing diversity of our workforce, we need to extend the practice of making employees feel valuable to those who work from a distance and across generations. Watch how your employees will respond to you if you convey to them these positive messages.

A friend recently forwarded an e-mail that supports this theme of human reactions and feelings. It related how an employee resolved a customer's problem with a thoughtful goodwill gesture that made the customer feel special. At the end of the story, my friend wrote: People may forget what you said; they may even forget what you did; but rarely, if ever, will they forget how you made them feel. (You'll find this reproduced in the Appendix.)

Regardless of distance, time, and technology, all contact is person to person. How do you want your employees to feel? Do you want them to feel special? Do you want them to feel that you genuinely care about them as people as well as producers? Do you want them to feel important? Do you want them to feel respected? Do you want them to feel trusted? Your answer to all these questions is probably, "Of course I do."

The most effective first step for creating these feelings in your employees is to take time to understand them. Understand their interests, their likes, their dislikes, their vulnerabilities, their hopes and dreams, their vocational aspirations, their pet peeves, and all the other characteristics that define them as the individuals they are. By understanding your employees and what drives them, you will increase employee motivation and loyalty.

Another friend, a member of a local garden club, was an expert on growing prize-winning orchids; his plants won first or second place in every horticultural contest he entered. Orchids are very delicate and challenging flowers to grow. When asked the secret of his horticultural successes, he said that he learned from books and other orchid growers precisely what these special plants needed from him to thrive. Then he created the atmosphere that enabled them to do just that.

Thus, it's simple to grow orchids when you provide them with what they need and check up on them to make sure the conditions are consistent with their requirements. This is particularly challenging when working in a virtual garden. Now, what special things can you do to take care of your "orchids"?

Share a Table for Two

When you get to know the people who report to you, you will form bonds that make it easier to communicate with them, to resolve differences, and to solve mutual problems. Those benefits will pay great dividends for both you and them.

The process of getting to know your employees might be a bit challenging given the multiple generational and global nature of today's workforce. Nonetheless, it begins with a genuine desire to learn all you can about each member of your staff and an interest in finding the best way of doing that. One way is to hold individual meetings (in person or remote if necessary) with each member of your staff. This is not a one-time investment but an ongoing process that will put you in personal contact several times with each person over the course of a few months. Initially, you may want to meet each member in person outside the office if possible. Later, you may limit the meetings to personal "touch base" meetings or discussions.

During a departmental meeting, simply tell your employees that you are interested in getting to know each of them and that you want them, in turn, to get to know you. Inform them that you will be "getting together" with everyone in the department, so that no one will feel singled out, and that the atmosphere will be informal, so that they do not feel anxious about the occasion. Let them know that you will agree on a schedule well in advance, so that they can plan accordingly, and that you are looking forward to these meetings, which should be both fun and interesting. At the end of your announcement, be sure to ask if anyone has any questions. Employees may well have concerns about the content of the meetings. They may wonder if you have a particular agenda in mind, since it is, sadly, rare that managers make such concerted efforts to get to know their staffs.

"Get to Know You" Questions

When meeting individually with your employees, remember that your objectives are to get to know your staff and to give them the opportunity to get to know you. You can accomplish this by asking direct questions, as you would in an interview, or by posing a problem or two—preferably real ones—and asking each person how he or she would deal with them. However you proceed, your approach should not be intimidating.

To set the stage for positive communication, make sure to tell your employees beforehand that you want to improve their work environment, their job satisfaction, and your abilities as a manager. Create a relaxed, casual environment conducive to open dialogue, even laughter, if possible.

Following are a few of the questions you may want to ask, although not necessarily in the form they are given. Always approach your interactions with your employees in a way that is natural to you. Disregard any questions with which you are uncomfortable, and, by all means, generate meaningful questions of your own.

- When you think about going to work, what do you look forward to doing? What excites and challenges you in your job?
- What, if anything, do you dread when you think about going to work?

- If you had a magic wand, what specifically would you change in our department? Why? What difference would that change make?
- I want to be the best manager I can be for you. What do you want me to know about you that would help me do that?
- What specifically do you need from me as your manager? (Then proceed to discuss each need in detail.)
- Will you describe for me the worst manager you ever had? What kinds of things did this manager do that made him or her the worst?
- Will you describe for me the best manager you ever had? What kinds of things did this manager do that made him or her the best?

Strategy for Asking Questions

Discussions of each one of the questions listed could take the better part of a lunch hour. For example, if you were to ask the last question, follow-up questions to the employee's initial response might be: How did specific things the manager did or said make you feel? Will you give me an example of how this manager handled problems that arose in the department? Were there certain qualities about this person that you liked? What were they?

Initial responses to each of these questions can stimulate more questions whose answers could, in turn, stimulate additional ones. Such in-depth discussions tell you a great deal about a person. Even if you delve into only one or two questions per meeting, as long as the discussion is informative and helps you know and understand the employee better than you did before, you have accomplished your goal.

Do not follow the same routine with each employee, to avoid giving the impression that each interview is identical. Instead, apply the concept of planned spontaneity. This means that you know in advance what you hope to gain from the meeting, you know where you want to begin (making sure you don't start off with the same question with each employee), and you allow the answer to each question to determine where you go with it. Planned spontaneity can lead you to beneficial discoveries and pleasant surprises. All you need to do is listen intently and ask appropriate questions. (The dos and don'ts of asking questions are the subject of a later chapter.) You may find that you spent the entire lunch hour examining only one of the questions you hoped to discuss. That's fine as long as you learned something valuable about your employee and vice versa.

Discovery Lesson

In your journal, list as many qualities you can think of that you would like your staff members to feel about you (e.g., respected, trusted, appreciated, important).

On a separate entry, for each feeling you listed, note your answer to this question: What specifically do I need to do to foster this feeling? Refer to this list of desirable behaviors as often as necessary throughout the course of your managerial career.

Questions to Consider

- *What other questions might I ask my employees during our meetings?*

   After meeting with employees:

- *What value did I gain from the discussions?*

- *Specifically, how can I use the knowledge I gained to help my employees be as productive as they can be?*

- *How can I show that I have actually assimilated their needs into the environment?*

People who give of themselves to others also give to themselves.

5

Clarifying What You and Your Employees Have in Common

YOU ARE A HUMAN BEING first and a manager second. Since your employees are also human beings first, you already have much in common with them. This means that your employees' expectations of you are not that much different from your expectations of your current manager or managers in the past. Likewise, your employees' desires of you (which are more than expectations) are not much different from the desires you have of your manager.

This realization should motivate you to treat your employees the way you would like to be treated. After all, while the differences between you and your staff might be more visible, the characteristics you have in common—your human characteristics—are far more significant. Specifically, some ways your employees might be different from you might include gender, race, geographic culture, and country of residence. However, sharpening your sense of how much you and the people under your influence have in common will differentiate you as a quality manager. Complete the following three-part discovery exercise to walk through the process of putting this into practice:

Discovery Lesson

1. Write your answer to this question: What, specifically, do I expect from my manager or the person to whom I report?

   Expectations in this context refer to all entitlements and any treatment you consider essential to performing your job. For example, it is reasonable for you to expect a respectful workplace and a clear understanding of what is required of you. These are essentials.

   If these and other minimal expectations were unfulfilled, you would be disappointed, unhappy, and probably inclined to look for other employment. Your value, effectiveness, and creativity can actually be eroded if your minimal expectations are ignored or belittled. Regardless, even if your minimal expectations were fulfilled, you would not be jumping up and down with excitement. More to the point, you would not be motivated to do your best; most likely, you would simply do whatever it took to get by. This is because it's normal for employees to give no more than they receive. That's the way it is with all perceived entitlements: it's no big deal to receive what you believe you have coming to you.

2. Now, write the answer to this question: What, specifically, do I desire from my manager?

   This list will be different from your list of expectations, because *desires, when fulfilled, are like unexpected bonuses or other pleasant surprises. We call them "It sure would be nice if _____ " items.* Some examples of desires are recognition for achievements that exceed your manager's expectations, challenges that recognize your skills, requests for your opinion, and any creative ways of being valued. Typically, when desires are fulfilled, employees extend themselves and perform above and beyond what's expected of them.

3. Review each of the two lists you just created, and answer this question: If my employees listed these same expectations and desires about me, how would I rate as a manager in fulfilling them consistently?

   If you hold certain expectations and desires of your manager, doesn't it stand to reason that your employees hold similar expectations and desires of you? Examine your notes and see for yourself if you are fulfilling your employees' possible expectations and desires.

To open the lines of communication between you and your employees, you need to elicit exactly what it is that they expect and desire of you. As noted in the Discovery Lesson, in many cases, their answers will not be much different from your own expectations and desires of your manager. However, each job and each employee carries a unique set of wants and desires, and it is to your benefit to find out what these are. The following is one way to do this, but you may choose a method of your own that produces the same positive results and communication.

Send a message (e-mail or other) to each of your employees requesting his or her comments on how you can improve on your performance as a manager. If you have only a few employees, you may want to talk with them directly instead. For example:

(E-mail) I want to be the best manager I can be for you. To do that, I'm enlisting your help. Please respond to the following five items and send your responses back within the week. Be completely honest—I'm trying to improve my performance as your manager, and your assistance is much needed and much appreciated.

1. Note specifically what you expect from me as your manager.
2. Concerning each of your expectations in question 1, on a scale of 1 (low) to 10, how *well* do I fulfill them?
3. Concerning each of your expectations in question 1, on a scale of 1 (low) to 10, how *consistently* do I fulfill them?
4. Complete the following sentence concerning your desires in as many ways as you would like: Although I don't expect it, it sure would be nice if you _____ .
5. Concerning each of the desires you mentioned in question 4, rate how important each is to you: 1 (very important), 2 (important), or 3 (slightly important).

Please include your name so that I can respond. And, in the spirit of helpfulness, feel free to add any other comments before sending it back.

When drafting your e-mail, be conscious of the language you use; regardless of your staff members' generation, culture, or gender, you want them to feel comfortable offering constructive criticism (see Chapter 11 on constructive criticism). Assure them that their responses will not detrimentally affect them or your treatment of them in the workplace.

Seriously evaluate the information and comments that your employees give you, with the knowledge that how effectively you motivate and manage people determines your managerial success. To fully benefit from what you learn, in your manager's journal make note of all of the expectations and desires that were expressed. You may find comments that occur repeatedly, in one way or another, from various people; pay particular attention to these. Next, determine specific ways in which you can fulfill these desires and expectations. Then record specific actions and solutions for future reference. It is important to note that all information is good information. It either tells you something about you or about the person who provided it. If the desires are unrealistic, it might encourage you to be clearer about what they can expect. That will help them true up their expectations with what they are experiencing.

Taking a proactive stance in improving your managerial capabilities will prove beneficial to your success as a manager and to the success of your department as a whole, no matter where the staff members are located.

Questions to Consider

- *What do my employees expect from me? How do I plan to fulfill and measure their reasonable expectations?*

- *What desires do my employees have of me? How do I plan to fulfill and measure those that are reasonable?*

continued

- *What benefits do I anticipate from answering the preceding questions?*

- *How do I respond to the employees' feedback to show them I listened and valued their input?*

PART II

Establishing a Solid Departmental Foundation

If someone were to ask you, "As manager of your department, what is your main overall objective?" you might say something like, "I want to build a strong and productive departmental structure." Few people would argue with that response. It's a goal that is not only reasonable but also achievable. The first step toward achieving your goal is to build a solid foundation, one that can support the departmental structure you want to create.

The cornerstone of such a foundation consists of five essential elements:

- Build trust
- Solicit feedback
- Inspire motivation
- Hone communication
- Expect and deliver quality

Building a foundation of which you will be proud is the subject of Part II. Each chapter provides an essential building block in the foundation of a problem-solving culture. Success in your managerial role is driven by how well you incorporate one or more of the five elements into your foundation. Some of the elements in this part are described below.

You will learn the effect of attitude on actions, both positive and negative. You will also learn that there is more to listening than meets the ear.

Responsive listening leads right to the art of asking questions. There are productive and destructive ways to ask questions. Productive questions will help you perpetuate open communication toward achieving the group's mission and objectives. Destructive questions will evoke defensiveness and send all those involved down a "weeded" path. Mastering the art of asking questions enables you to effectively connect with your employees and help them solve problems.

You will also learn to constructively criticize employees so that they view the criticism as a gift. All too often, criticisms are confused with adverse judgments. The intent of the former is to be helpful and foster improvement, while the intent of the latter is to highlight shortcomings. For criticisms to be received as gifts, they have to be properly packaged and presented.

That brings us back to helping you adopt the right attitude and intent when you are delivering them.

An attitude is a state of mind and a predisposition to actions based on what you tell yourself.

Attitudes precede actions; positive attitudes lead to productive actions; negative attitudes lead to unproductive actions. Adopt and encourage positive attitudes.

6

Adopting Positive and Productive Attitudes

LET'S SAY YOU'VE BEEN INVITED to a meeting which you really don't want to go to but for obligatory reasons you must attend. You don't have a choice of whether or not to accept the invitation, but you can choose your attitude regarding it.

By attitude, we mean a state of mind—an emotional and intellectual inclination—and a predisposition to actions based on what you tell yourself. In the case of the meeting, if you were to choose a negative attitude, you would not participate and would make sure the meeting is not valuable or productive for you. That's because you would tell yourself, "I really don't want to go to this meeting because I know nothing will change and they will ask for my input and ignore it anyway."

Conversely, if you chose a positive attitude, you would feel better about going because you would tell yourself, "I am not sure this is the best use of my time, but as long as I have to go, I will see if I can learn something I might have missed out on had I not been invited."

In all likelihood, whichever attitude you chose would result in your prediction coming true. This phenomenon is called the self-fulfilling prophecy. When we have a strong belief about the outcome of a relationship or an impending experience, we do everything in our power to make that belief come true.

It would not be an overstatement to say that our attitudes are responsible for creating, and even perpetuating, our joys and sorrows, our good and bad times, our successes and failures, and the quality of our relationships.

Since attitudes are powerful keys to your success as a manager, this chapter explains the nature of attitudes and how you can use positive attitudes to create a fertile departmental culture.

The Three Key Elements of Attitudes

The first element of attitude is what you tell yourself. As an activity, talking to yourself is neither good nor bad. We all do it. However, what you tell yourself can determine whether the consequences of your self-talk will be productive or destructive.

The effect of self-talk on behavior is evident every day of our lives, both at work and at home. The good news about self-talk is that you can hear it and then compare it with what you really want from a given situation or relationship.

The second element of attitude involves having a clear idea in your mind of what you want or need. When you are conscious about what you want from a person, situation, or relationship, you can control what you tell yourself. Often what you tell yourself initially is reactive, but if you stop at that point to think about what you want, you can adjust the intent of your "internal dialogue" to support and reinforce what you want or need. This censoring process is very valuable in all volatile or important situations. Consider the following examples of these elements.

Several years ago, I was teaching a graduate class called Training and Development. One of the requirements was that each student teach the rest of the class to do something at which the presenter was competent.

About two weeks earlier, one of my students, Marla, was due to conduct her teaching session, and she came to me with a problem. "I get panicky whenever I have to make a presentation, either in class or at work," she said. "And because I get panicky, I always fail at this task. I don't want to fail anymore. I don't want to fail this class. What can I do to overcome my fear?"

I asked her what she tells herself just before making a presentation. "Nothing. I'm not aware of telling myself anything," she said.

"But you must," I insisted. "Think of the last time you had to make a presentation, and tell me about how you felt just before you had to do it."

She replied that a month ago she was required to present the results of a market research study she conducted to her company's advertising and sales departments. This report was to provide valuable insights for developing the company's marketing campaign.

She said, "I was really nervous and was sure they would find fault with my conclusions. I thought they would make fun of my presentation. I was also scared they would ask me questions I wouldn't be able to answer."

After she relayed all of this negative self-talk, I asked her what happened. She said, "Most of my fears came true. My presentation was a flop. My presentations are always a flop. That's why I'm afraid of putting on a training session for the class."

What she had chosen for the assignment was to teach her fellow students how to prepare an effective résumé. I asked, "Do you consider the skills you want to impart to the students important and valuable?"

"Yes, of course," she said.

"Then, this is what I want you to tell yourself a couple of days before your presentation: 'I am about to give this class a gift—one from which they will benefit. They will be better off for receiving this gift, and they will thank me for giving it to them. I am glad that I have the opportunity to share my knowledge with them.'"

An hour before her presentation, Marla came into my office to tell me how excited she was about the impending training session. "I really believe I'm about to give the class a gift they will cherish, and I'm looking forward to it. I wanted to come by to thank you," she said.

Marla's presentation was well received. She was poised, confident, and organized. She focused on the information she was giving her students rather than on how they might receive her. Her actual performance, thus, was a clear example of a positive self-fulfilling prophecy.

The power of what people tell themselves is evident in another case, this one involving the customer service department of a former client, a medium-size manufacturing firm in the Midwest.

According to this client's vice president of operations, the company's customer service department was the object of frequent complaints. Specifically, people said they were treated rudely by customer service representatives, were left on hold for what seemed to be forever, were disconnected while waiting to be helped, and were not given the help they hoped to receive. These complaints, which were not offset by compliments, went on for about a year and were accompanied by a steady decline in sales.

When I met with the five-person department, I asked, "When the phone rings, what do you tell yourself before you answer it?" Every person related a variation of the same negative self-talk: "I wonder what this jerk wants" or "Oh, hell, here comes another complainer."

After discussing with the group the effect of self-talk on behaviors, I suggested they tell themselves something else when the phone rings. For instance: "The caller has a problem, which is why he or she is calling"; "My job is to help each caller with his or her problem and I can do that"; "I am a valuable aid to people who are in trouble."

As part of the solution, they also adopted the greeting "How can I help you?" when answering the phone. This simple question was more than words. It was a genuine positive attitude, revealed in their tone of voice and helpful actions that said, in effect, "I care about your problem and have a sincere desire to help you."

Within a month, the vice president of operations started to receive calls from customers praising the customer service department's services.

The third element is intent. If your intent is to harm or be negative, it will come through. However, if your intent is to help, learn, or grow, it can also help to adjust your attitude. So, let's play this out in a simple example.

Situation: One of your key employees did not meet the deadline for an assignment you gave him.

First round of self-talk: "That guy is irresponsible and worthless. If I wanted it late, I could have done it myself."

Want or need: I need that employee to be productive and timely, and I do not want to upset him, but I do need to get him to be more timely.

Second round of self-talk: "How can I get that guy to be more timely with his assignments? I wonder why they are always late?"

Intent: I am curious not accusatory, and I desire to be productive not destructive.

Perhaps you can give some thought to how the results with an improved attitude might be different from those that would have resulted from the initial attitude.

The three elements are interdependent: what you tell yourself creates thoughts and feelings, what you want tempers those thoughts and feelings with something rational, which makes room for making sure your intent is clear as well. When they are all aligned, the actions are in line as well. Therefore, to change what you tell yourself and the resulting actions, you must adjust and align your attitudes.

In general, positive attitudes, such as genuine caring or love, lead to helpful actions, whereas negative attitudes, such as unreasonable fear and anger, lead to defensive behaviors.

Following are three examples of how these elements work together when you give yourself positive messages.

Example 1

What you tell yourself: I am a student of everybody.

Aligned attitudes: Inquisitive; curious; receptive to learning; respectful of "teachers."

Actions: Ask appropriate questions; listen attentively; express appreciation for the teacher's time and attention.

Example 2

What you tell yourself: I am a human being first, a manager second.

Aligned attitudes: Caring and compassionate; sensitive; considerate and thoughtful.

Actions: Listen attentively; offer help when needed; be reasonably flexible.

Example 3

What you tell yourself: For every symptom there is a cause. If possible, don't treat symptoms, such as poor performance; determine the cause and then deal appropriately with the problem.

Aligned attitudes: Viewing poor performance as a problem-solving challenge; probing for possible causes of the symptoms; making a commitment to finding a solution to the problem; challenging yourself to help the person find direction.

Actions: Ask appropriate questions; weigh alternative solutions to the problem; work with the employee to resolve the problem; encourage the employee to develop a positive attitude toward resolving the problem.

To reinforce a strong relationship among the three elements of attitude, do this: Every time you're feeling angry or hostile toward an employee, a customer, or anyone else who is important to you, ask yourself, "What do I want, and what am I telling myself that could be causing this negative reaction?" Once you've identified what you're telling yourself that's fostering this negativity, come up with a statement to yourself that could alter your state of mind.

For example, you might be angry with a particular employee for not doing what you asked. To change this negative thought, you should consider whether or not the employee was aware of your explicit expectations. Is it possible that you did not properly convey your expectations and have been operating under the erroneous assumption that your employee knew what was required of him? Since that is a possibility, you would simply ask your employee if you had told him what you expected from him. If properly phrased in a nonthreatening manner that doesn't make him feel as if he is under attack, your question should lead to an open dialogue with potential positive outcomes. The best way to do it is to start with *you* owning the problem by saying, "I am not sure I explained what I needed from you. Can we talk about it?" This always leads to better communication and understanding between your employee and yourself.

Similarly, you might have someone in your department whom you consider to be a bad seed. Perhaps this person upsets the positive exchange of information within the group through defensiveness or a negative attitude. By merely observing that your employee is a bad seed, you do nothing to amend the situation. You need to take an active approach. Perhaps this person doesn't feel as if she fits in with the group. If this is the case, how might you encourage a sense of teamwork and cooperation? Asking questions, with an attitude of wanting to better understand the cause, provides a guide for the appropriate next steps.

Be more aware of your approach to interpersonal communications with your employees by replacing passive and negative thoughts with active and positive ones on a daily basis. Then observe what happens.

Creating a Fertile Departmental Culture

To create and perpetuate a fertile departmental culture, encourage all employees to adopt attitudes that will enable them to be productive, to perform their jobs conscientiously, and to act professionally toward their co-workers, customers, vendors, and even competitors. You do this by incorporating what we call the positive attitude adoption program. This program is a three-phase process that requires the cooperation and contributions of all your employees.

Phase 1

The objective of this phase is to compile a list of attitudes that reflect the values of everyone in your department. The two attitudes heading your list should be respectfulness and trustworthiness, which are the foundations of any meaningful relationship, be it personal or professional.

First you will need to bring your department together, whether in a conference room, on a conference call, or through a Net meeting. Before the meeting, tell your employees that, in the interest of creating a fertile departmental culture that promotes employees' personal development and productivity, you are planning to initiate a positive attitude adoption program. You will probably need to define what an attitude is and then inform your department members that the two attitudes that will head your list are respectfulness and trustworthiness. Ask them to bring to the meeting a list of attitudes that they would like the department to adopt. During the meeting, discuss the attitudes presented by your staff, and agree on a final list.

Phase 2

In a follow-up meeting, for every attitude that you believe should be adopted, agree on how it could be converted into actions. Here is a composite list of "respectful" behaviors that were arrived at by several of our clients:

- Listen attentively without interruption and make an effort to understand what is being said.
- Express gratitude when appropriate.
- Find value in any criticism you receive.
- Be polite.

- Ask for opinions and seriously consider those opinions.
- Be considerate of each employee's feelings.
- Cooperate with each other because, even though we are a diverse, global community, we have common objectives.
- Celebrate each other's achievements and extend sincere, specific compliments when appropriate.
- Return phone calls and e-mail messages as promptly as possible.
- Be forthright and compassionate in dealing with fellow employees.
- Extend yourself to fulfill customers' needs and their reasonable expectations.
- Have fun; enjoy what you do.

Feel free to include these behaviors when compiling your department's list. If you like, you can create several different lists of respectful behaviors. One list could comprise behaviors toward fellow employees, while another could emphasize behaviors toward customers and still another might represent respectful behaviors that each individual should do for himself or herself.

Your second list of positive departmental behaviors should demonstrate qualities of trustworthiness. At the top of your department's list should be: "Act responsibly—fulfill all promises, and don't make promises that the employee or department can't keep." Without this element of trustworthiness, the company's reputation among its clients and in the industry could be diminished. Other exemplary behaviors that appeared on many of our clients' lists were: maintain each other's confidence; do not judge each other's feelings; be sincere; and verify what is needed and what will be delivered.

Your list of trustworthy behaviors along with your lists of respectful behaviors will serve as a good start to achieve a positive departmental culture. As time permits, generate lists of behaviors that reflect the other attitudes you and your staff agreed to adopt.

Phase 3

In your final meeting in the series, decide as a group how you can reinforce the agreed-on attitudes and the behaviors that reflect them. More specifically, how should you respond when a co-worker's behavior violates an attitude you agreed to adopt? One way is to be forthright and remind the offender that he or she agreed to abide by your departmental creed. However the reminder is expressed, it should be a gentle nudge and not a hit over the head with a brick.

Discovery Lesson

To discover for yourself the relationship between what you tell yourself and what you do, complete this two-part exercise.

1. Come up with a negative statement about someone you know, using the person's name. Write this statement on a sheet of paper or in your manager's journal, and then read it aloud. Next, write down all the possible attitudes you could harbor toward this person that were triggered by the negative statement. Finally, write down all the actions that could result from your attitudes.

   Example: John is insensitive toward his fellow employees. He seems not to care when he puts someone on the spot publicly. When he is told what he does and the effect it has on people, he says, "They are overly sensitive."

   Attitudes I harbor toward John: No matter what I'd say or do, John would not pay attention to me. I really don't like John because he's disrupting my department. I can't trust John with projects that require him to work with others.

   Actions that could result from my negative attitudes toward John: I don't make a concerted effort to help John realize how he's affecting

continued

the department. I ignore John and allow others to follow my lead. I keep him isolated from the rest of the department.

2. Now come up with a positive statement about someone you know, again using the person's name. Follow the same procedure as you did in the first part of this exercise.

Example: Mary is conscientious and wants to succeed.

Attitudes I harbor toward Mary: She is a great addition to the department. Mary can be counted on to help anyone in the department who needs it. Because she's eager to learn, I want to help her in any way I can so she'll succeed. I'm eager to have her represent our department at major meetings with other departments.

Actions that result from my positive attitudes toward Mary: I include her in any project that could benefit from her expertise. I use her as a mentor for new employees requiring special attention. I go out of my way to teach her what I know.

What you should have discovered from this exercise is that positive attitudes lead to productive actions and negative attitudes lead to unproductive actions. To be a successful, professional manager, encourage positive attitudes from all members of your department.

Questions to Consider

- *People who have positive attitudes tend to look at the whole. Those with negative attitudes do not see the W—they tend to focus on the hole. As a manager, one of your obligations is to teach your employees to add Ws in their lives. Therefore, how can you fulfill this obligation?*

- *Suppose you have a person in your department whose actions reflect a negative attitude? What specifically can you do to help this person alter his or her actions?*

> *Remove all limiting beliefs and excuses for achieving success.*
>
> *If it is to be, it's up to me.*

7

Perpetuating a Problem-Solving Culture

WHEN A WELL-REGARDED COMPANY PRESIDENT was asked to explain the secret of his success, he said, "I remove any excuses my employees might have for not performing well by giving them everything they need to perform to the best of their abilities. I don't want to be anyone's excuse for not fulfilling responsibilities. Without excuses, those who don't have the desire to succeed will leave."

Working within a problem-solving culture becomes increasingly more important as our work responsibilities swell at a quicker rate than our time to accomplish the resulting tasks. Knowing your team members can count on each other to focus on issues in a healthy, collaborative way will keep your team moving in a positive direction while each member juggles all these day-to-day challenges.

You have the power to create either a problem-solving culture or a toxic culture. The way you tackle problems and interact with others sets the tone for your employees, telling them what kind of person you are, what type of departmental culture you want to cultivate, and what you expect of them in similar situations.

A problem-solving culture is based on productive resolution and respect. Conversely, a toxic culture is a fear-based environment where people are more concerned about protecting themselves than solving problems.

In this chapter, we provide a framework for assessing, articulating, and resolving problems in a problem-solving manner. We contrast that with what one might experience within a toxic culture. Understanding these dynamics and how they occur in these very different cultures will provide a useful frame of reference as you seek to build your own problem-solving culture.

What Is a Problem?

A problem is a *perceived divergence* between a reasonable want, need, or expectation and what has happened or is happening. Since the perception belongs to the person with the problem, the problem belongs to that person as well. To prove the practical validity of this explanation, recall two or three major problems you have encountered recently at work. Concerning each problem, answer the following two questions: What made it a problem? What did you want or need that you lacked? Almost always, your answer to both questions will be essentially the same. The reason it was a problem was because *you* were not getting what you *needed, wanted, or expected.*

How do you know you have a problem? You know you have a problem when you observe symptoms—deviations from your expected normality that bother you. Symptoms are subtle indications, behaviors, or results that tell you something is not quite right or is not the way you want it to be. For example, symptoms of an unhealthy plant include drooping leaves, leaves turning yellow, and edges of leaves turning brown. The situation is "the plant is not getting what it needs to be healthy." The problem is, "I want a healthy plant and this one is not."

Similarly, when you have a low-grade fever and a runny nose and are inordinately tired or unusually irritable, you are exhibiting symptoms of a cold or perhaps something more complicated. The situation is you are not feeling well. The problem is you want to feel better, but you don't. Being aware of symptoms and having a keen ability to recognize them is important because they are potentially red flags that signal either an impending problem or an existing problem.

Recognizing you may have a problem in your department or with an employee, or that you are on the verge of encountering one, is a prerequisite to solving it. One word of caution: be careful not to mistake a symptom for a problem. Symptoms are indications of a potential problem, not problems themselves.

Let's look at the characteristics of a problem-solving culture, and then we'll apply the concepts in the examples following.

Characteristics of a Problem-Solving Culture

In a problem-solving culture, managers and team members understand that their main functions as a group is to solve problems and produce results. It is the manager's role to set a tone of collaborative, resolution-based fact finding. Team members should know to ask themselves the following diagnostic questions whenever a problem arises:

Diagnostic Problem-Solving Questions

- What specifically do I want? Is it reasonable (i.e., attainable)?
- Am I committed to resolving the problem methodically and conscientiously?
- If negative thoughts or outside influences are sidetracking me, what specifically can I do to rid myself of those thoughts and influences?

In a problem-solving culture, these questions enable employees to progress from articulating a problem through a methodical, cohesive effort to find a solution.

Let's review five situations you might encounter as a manager. Each one contains a description of the situation followed by the problem stated in positive terms. To bring about resolution, you must first frame a problem and present it to your employees in positive terms. Proper presentation of a problem statement includes two key attributes:

- It states what you need, want, or expect and is based on what is currently happening, or what you wish to happen, but is not.
- It is stated in positive terms.

Situation: You have a staff member whose contributions are substantially less than what she is capable of giving.

Problem statement: *You need* her to contribute at an agreed level and she is not.

Situation: Two staff members need to work together, but they don't like each other and would rather not be teamed.

Furthermore, their mutual dislike is adversely affecting their performance.

Problem statement: *You want* them to get along; *you need* them to work together; and *you expect* them to accomplish their work and they are not.

Situation: An employee is overly sensitive and becomes defensive when you or other members of the department correct him or attempt to help him.

Problem statement: *You need* him to accept feedback constructively; *you want* him to trust you and his co-workers and he does not.

Situation: You have a staff member who is constantly complaining. For her, the glass is almost always half empty.

Problem statement: *You need* her to adopt a positive attitude or offer productive solutions and she is not.

Situation: A high-performing employee who was highly motivated had a recent deterioration in his demeanor and a decline in his performance.

Problem statement: *You need* him to be a high performer again; *you expect* him to deliver; *you want* to understand what happened and why, but you cannot . . . yet.

You may have noticed we italicized some text; what is common about what we italicized? A surprising but essential point to accept is that every problem you have is *your* responsibility. This is true even though, as in the examples above, you could identify a particular employee who was the source. It is your problem because what you're seeing is a deviation from *your* desires, requirements, and expectations and what is happening. Therefore, you must take responsibility for solving it as well as any other problems that arise in your department.

Note the importance of both key attributes. Even when you take ownership, but do not state it in positive terms, the problem comes out as a complaint. Compare, for example, the following two statements.

Situation: Joe's performance has deteriorated over the past month.

- "My problem is that Joe's performance for the past month has been deteriorating."
- "I need to understand why Joe is not performing as I expected and help him improve going forward."

The first statement is nothing more than a complaint. The second, which portrays the case in positive terms with ownership, displays a desire and interest in enabling the resolution. Whenever employees deliver problems to you stated in negative terms, as a complaint, you need to receive them and respond by raising three proactive, positive questions: What do they specifically want or need that they do not currently have? Why is this happening? And what actions can they take to solve the problem with or without your assistance? These proactive questions will stimulate problem-solving attitudes and reinforce corresponding problem-solving skills among your employees.

In the preceding example, the answer is, "I need to understand why Joe's performance has deteriorated during the last month so we can arrive at some ways to help him improve."

How Do I Resolve a Problem?

Having a positive attitude with a desire for understanding of why the situation exists and what is causing the problem provides a direction and a strategy for remedying it. Remember, you cannot always fix the cause, but knowing the cause provides insight on figuring out how to remedy or productively manage the resulting problem. A resolution statement to that problem always starts with an implicit or explicit question of, "What do I still need to understand about the situation based on the symptoms?"

Let's revisit the earlier examples.

Situation: You have a staff member whose contributions are substantially less than what she is capable of giving.

Problem statement: *You need* her to contribute at an agreed level and she is not.

Resolution questions: Why is she not fulfilling her potential? What courses of action are available to help her and you resolve this problem?

Situation: Two staff members need to work together, but they don't like each other and would rather not be teamed. Furthermore, their mutual dislike is adversely affecting their performance.

Problem statement: *You want* them to get along; *you need* them to work together; and *you expect* them to accomplish their work and they are not.

Resolution questions: Why are they at odds? How can you help them foster more positive attitudes toward each other that will lead to mutual cooperation and respect?

Situation: An employee is overly sensitive and becomes defensive when you or other members of the department correct him or attempt to help him.

Problem statement: *You need* him to accept feedback constructively; *you want* him to trust you and his co-workers and he does not.

Resolution questions: Why is he defensive? What can you do to help him understand and receive feedback more constructively?

Situation: You have a staff member who is constantly complaining. For her, the glass is almost always half empty.

Problem statement: *You need* her to adopt a positive attitude or offer productive solutions and she is not.

Resolution questions: What are the reasons for this negativity? Are there ways of getting this employee to view things differently?

Situation: A high-performing employee who was highly motivated had a recent deterioration in his demeanor and a decline in his performance.

Problem statement: *You need* him to be a high performer again; *you expect* him to deliver; *you want* to understand what happened and you cannot.

Resolution questions: Why the sudden change? What can you do to help him resolve his concerns?

What do all the resolution questions have in common? They all reflect a desire to understand the situation in order to move toward solutions. By adopting attitudes that produce a positive working environment you will set an example and set the stage for developing mutually rewarding relationships between you and your employees and thus build a problem-solving culture.

Although we want to strive for a problem-solving culture, we realize managers are often faced with people and behaviors that are reflective of a toxic culture. However, now that you are armed with the knowledge of how powerful a problem-solving culture can be, we will present the stark contrast with a toxic culture. As you read through the next section, feel the difference. We will compare them at the end.

Characteristics of a Toxic Culture

Warning! Danger! Beware! The following explanation presents attitudes and behaviors that are dangerous to the problem-solving culture. If anything in the following section sounds like you or your current environment, you can be sure you are working in or fostering a toxic culture.

How do potentially good managers create such a bad culture? Obviously, it's not intentional. No manager we know starts the morning saying, "I wonder what I can do today to create a toxic department." Nor does any manager we know say, "What can I do to cause my employees to be afraid of me and of each other?" Nevertheless, their words and actions do both.

The dominant and pervasive attitude of employees in a toxic culture is paralyzing fear: fear of expressing opinions, taking risks, being adversely judged, being misunderstood, being wrongly penalized, and doing or saying anything they feel might threaten their position or image. Because employees are fearful, their number one objective is to protect themselves from getting emotionally hurt and from tarnishing their image.

Sometimes, to make themselves look good, employees will undermine and find fault with others. Worse, they harbor variations of such attitudes as "Every man for himself," "It's a dog-eat-dog world," and "I do what's best for me." The result of these negative mind-sets is that "I" takes precedence over "we." Since a department is by definition a collective group of individuals, this negative mind-set does nothing to maintain or advance the productivity of the group and is inevitably detrimental to your department.

Many of the conversations in defensive office cultures are personal and tainted with accusatory language such as "You are . . . ,"

"You don't . . . ," "You never . . . ," and "You always . . ." followed by negative phrases that can put people on the defensive. Blaming, finding fault, making excuses, holding grudges, and spreading negative rumors are also prevalent. These are not necessarily signs of bad apples in your department, but they are all unhealthy expressions of insecurity and trepidation.

Managers and other employees in such cultures are so caught up with their inordinate need to be right and to look good that they fail to see the consequences of their egocentric and defensive attitudes. In reality, these attitudes are like weeds, which rob gardens of vital nutrients. A weed-infested department stifles creativity, discourages innovative thinking, and stunts the growth and development of its employees.

Following are several common ways in which managers of defensive cultures spread their negative influence.

- They are judgmental and engage in character assassinations. Judgments essentially say, implicitly or explicitly, "You don't know what you're talking about," "Your opinions and beliefs are not worthy of consideration," "Your attitude is terrible," or even "You're a fool." Character assassinations typically begin with "You" or "Your," followed by a negative comment. By making such a pat statement about an individual, managers are being judgmental.

- They believe they have all the answers and do not value their employees' contributions. The actions of these defensive managers, as well as their words, communicate the attitude "If you don't see things the same way I do, there is something wrong with you" or "I have all the answers." Managers who convey these attitudes stifle give-and-take between themselves and their employees. They also discourage employees from contributing their knowledge and experience and make them feel guilty for making mistakes.

- They make employees feel stupid for asking questions or sharing ideas. An old saying tells us that there are no stupid questions. In fact, if you want to know the answer to a question, it's stupid not to ask. By discouraging employees from asking questions or presenting ideas, whether this is stated or conveyed through negative reactions, a manager fails in one of the job's main functions: to be a teacher. This message causes employees to be afraid to take risks, even reasonable ones. Since all progress requires a certain amount of risk, instilling a fear of taking risks and of making mistakes is tantamount to preventing employees from growing.

- They dignify defensiveness by allowing an employee to blame others for failing to fulfill his or her own responsibilities, by accepting excuses as substitutes for facts, or by condoning behaviors that do not serve the best interests of the department. Actions that do not lead a person at least one step closer to meeting reasonable objectives are ineffective. Accepting scapegoating, excuses, or counterproductive behavior does not solve problems. On the contrary, it impedes the problem-solving process.

- They are disrespectful toward their employees. Respect and trust are the framework of any good relationship. Any action that does not consider the feelings of employees or that is not responsive to their need to be trusted demonstrates a lack of concern for them as people. An employee who meets with this reaction will likely not feel the need to live up to a higher standard and, moreover, will likely not respect the manager who behaves in this fashion.

- They fail to fulfill their promises or deny that they made promises. Breaking promises not only conveys a noncaring, insensitive attitude but also says to others that being untrustworthy is an acceptable behavior. Imagine if this were what employees learned from you, and then imagine what would happen if they were to carry these same negative behaviors over to their interactions with your customers. If employees repeatedly promise customers that they will receive a product by a certain date and then fail to follow through on these promises, you will find your customer base quickly decreasing. Instead, by setting a higher standard for members of your department, you encourage similar behavior on their part and garner their trust.

- They breed negativity by accentuating what is wrong with the department, playing favorites, and speaking badly of employees to other members of the department. By harping on the negative aspects of a department, managers drive employees to play the "blame game" rather than finding ways to fix the problems so the department is more productive. By playing favorites, they exclude all nonfavorite members of the group and stir negative feelings throughout. Employees who are not receiving encouragement and supervision will not live up to their highest potential and will end up resenting the manager's "pets," while those receiving all of the manager's attention may feel entitled to benefits they did not earn and may perceive themselves as above working with and listening to their fellow employees. In the same vein, speaking badly of employees not only sets a bad example but also creates divisiveness among the staff.

All of these defensive actions have certain traits in common. First, not one of these behaviors will consistently help managers or their employees solve problems. Second, they deter employees from being as productive as they can be. Remember, actions or reactions that do not lead managers or their employees one step closer to a reasonable want—a want that serves the best interests of the department—are defensive behaviors. Finally, defensive behaviors block people, and thus an entire department, from steadily moving forward. Such behaviors may have short-term value and achieve short-term results, but in the journey to success, habitual defensiveness is a dead end.

Helping Employees Learn the Problem-Solving Model

Now you have learned about both the problem-solving culture and the toxic culture. Assuming you want to perpetuate the more productive culture, consider what happens when your staff member, Harry, comes to you and says, "I've got a problem and I need your help." You can provide him assistance in framing and solving his problem through the three-step process. This process reflects the basic philosophy of a problem-solving culture, which is that all employees are worthy of respect. A good manager respects employees' emotions, options, and abilities to solve problems on their own or with some coaching.

Remember that a problem is a deviation between what happened and what was desired or expected. So the first step is to encourage Harry to present the symptoms with the intent of understanding the root cause and the deviation. If Harry is upset about an incident, ask him to describe it in concrete terms; the more specific the better. Second, he already said he has a problem. He owns it. So, given the symptoms, help him frame his problem using positive terms.

Once you understand what the problem is, you can help him assess options. Ask what he might do to solve the problem. Discuss alternative solutions with him, and, if necessary, bring some options to his attention and then discuss with him the pros and cons of each. Through this process you are modeling problem-solving strategies and thereby creating a path for success.

Remember the well-regarded company president who was asked to explain the secret of his success? He said, "I remove any excuses they might have for not performing well by giving them everything they need to perform to the best of their abilities. I don't want to be anyone's excuse for not fulfilling responsibilities. Without excuses, those who don't have the desire to succeed will leave."

We have heard variations of this philosophy during our years of consulting with companies whose managers succeeded in creating problem-solving cultures. The main attitude each of them had in common is a genuine regard for the people under their influence. They want them to succeed. So they do whatever is necessary to help them achieve their objectives. Their genuine caring attitude is expressed in a variety of ways. With both their words and actions they communicate that, as members of the team, employees are vital and valuable contributors. These successful managers also provide employees with the tools and resources required for them to succeed.

The following are some of the specific attitudes and actions that successful managers we've known encourage in their departments and companies:

- Be willing to take risks.
- Be helpful to fellow employees.
- Own the problem-solving process (as opposed to blaming others for causing the problems).
- Be trustworthy.
- Be a conscientious student of your fellow employees and the people you serve, because everyone has something to teach.
- Avoid asking questions that place people on the defensive.
- Be sensitive toward others.

Compare toxic cultures with problem-solving cultures and you will invariably find that the former stifle productivity and growth, while the latter encourage employees to be the best they can be. This comparison clearly demonstrates why problem-solving managers are successful.

Comparing Toxic and Problem-Solving Cultures

Toxic Cultures	*Problem-Solving Cultures*
• Characterized by fearful attitudes.	• Characterized by genuine caring attitudes.
• Manager has all the answers.	• Manager asks astute questions; manager is a student of the employees.
• People are mainly concerned with who is right.	• People are mainly concerned with what is right.
• People focus on personalities.	• People focus on issues and solutions.
• People ask questions that place others on the defensive.	• People ask questions that lead to solutions.
• Risk taking is discouraged.	• Risk taking is encouraged.
• Problems are stated in negative terms.	• Problems are stated in positive terms.
• People complain about what they're not getting.	• People ask: "How can I accomplish X so I can get Y?"
• People view themselves as victims.	• People view themselves as being in control of their problems.
• People are resistant to change.	• People are responsive to change.
• People are close-minded.	• People are open-minded.

Discovery Lesson 1

Problem-Solving Culture: Identify three problems you encountered in the last week. See if you can break them out by using a situation statement, a problem statement, and a resolution question. Now reflect back to see how this methodical approach is different from what your tactics might have been in the heat of the moment. What do you see?

Discovery Lesson 2

Toxic Culture: If you are going to lead by example, then you should do all you can to minimize your own defensiveness. This Discovery Lesson is based on the notion that awareness is the beginning of change.

Listen carefully to people talking to each other, either at meetings or in casual conversations. Every time you hear what you deem an important conversation that is sprinkled with defensive statements, record the conversation in writing as soon as you can. Describe the scene, the people present, and the subject of the conversation, as well as actual statements. Do this for a few days. Then transfer your notes to your manager's journal, and label the section "Defensive Statements I Overheard and What They Really Mean."

For each negative statement you noted, ask yourself these questions: Will this statement move the speaker one step closer to achieving a reasonable want? What is the point of the defensive statement?

continued

What does the speaker hope to accomplish? Will the speaker succeed in getting whatever it is he or she wants, which is really important to this person?

In most cases, you'll recognize that the negative statements you overheard are a waste of time, energy, and emotion. This is because defensiveness of any sort may satisfy one's emotions, but it doesn't resolve the problem that triggered the defensiveness. The only thing that was accomplished was that the employee blew off some steam.

Questions to Consider

- *How can I better transform situations I encounter into problems I can solve?*

- *How can I encourage my employees to be problem solvers rather than defenders?*

- *How can I model my attitudes and behaviors so that I don't inadvertently do anything to create a toxic culture in my department?*

- *When I encounter toxic behavior, how can I approach it with problem-solving attitudes?*

Every action or reaction communicates something. Determining what each "something" is provides the enlightenment to understand and respond with clarity, care, and purpose.

8

Listening—*Really* Listen and You Will Hear More than Words

A WELL-KNOWN SYMPHONY CONDUCTOR WAS holding auditions for a new pianist. One particular candidate came highly recommended. In fact, many of the orchestra's supporters were sure he would be selected because of his mastery of the keyboard. To no one's surprise, the candidate played flawlessly at the audition. However, he was not selected. The disappointed supporters asked the conductor why he declined to hire this pianist, given that he had played the composition perfectly. The maestro said, "It is true that this pianist played all the notes exactly as they were written. And, while that is important, we are looking for someone who sees beyond the notes as well. We are looking for someone who will play the music." Everyone understood the decision instantly. Precision should not be mistaken for passion.

Listening Is More than Hearing

Effective listening is more complex and more important than ever before. Experts used to say that, more than just the act of hearing, true listening involves thinking and processing. With increases in technology leading to fewer face-to-face meetings, listening may now require reading, writing, hearing, watching, seeing, processing, and questioning. As you read on, attach all of those actions to the word *listen*.

How do tone and actions present a more accurate picture than words alone can convey? Have you ever asked someone how they are doing and he responds, "I am just fine," yet his arms are crossed and he is looking anywhere but at you. Or have you ever received an e-mail written in ALL CAPITAL LETTERS? The "I'm fine" example is a common one, and, intentional or not, an e-mail written in all capital letters is usually interpreted as yelling. So, tune in and listen; it's worth it.

When you listen to your staff members, listen for the music, not just the notes. Listen for the feelings, not just the facts. Listen not only to what is said or written but also to the way it is said or presented. Be careful, however, not to let differences in communication styles and tools skew or hide the true tone of the messages you are receiving. In short, listen for context. Listen to the tone of the words as well as to the words themselves. Then, make sure you heard it right. Verifying tone is essential in maintaining trust and effective communication.

The Intent Is in the Tone—Verify It

Emphasis placed on specific words, speed of the delivery, volume, and the pitch of one's voice all change the tone of what is said. To demonstrate, read this sentence aloud: I can't believe he didn't select that pianist.

Now change the emphasis of the individual words as indicated:

I can't believe he didn't select that pianist.

I **can't** believe he didn't select that pianist.

I can't **believe** he didn't select that pianist.

I can't believe **he** didn't select that pianist.

I can't believe he **didn't** select that pianist.

I can't believe he didn't **select** that pianist.

I can't believe he didn't select **that** pianist.

I can't believe he didn't select that **pianist.**

The notes are the same, but the music is different. Simple changes in emphasis can produce dramatic alterations in how the sentence is heard.

How do you and your employees talk or exchange messages? Think about it. Are your tones supportive? Intimidating? Aggressive? Confrontational? Friendly? Something else? Is technology affecting things? Listen for the tone in what your employees say to determine the mood and motivation behind each statement. And if you are not sure, ask!

Many people believe only facts are necessary. However, even instant messaging has developed a whole language around expressing feelings during exchanges because it reveals the emotion behind the words. That is where the depth and body of the message really resides. You cannot presume to know what your employees are thinking; the facts aren't enough. You need to sense the feelings and motivations behind the words. And remember, for every one of us, it's the feelings, the emotions, that drive our behavior.

How do your employees feel about you and about each other? How do they feel about their jobs? About what you ask them to do? About your methods of handling problems? If you listen—really listen—you'll detect the clues that will help you answer these questions. You'll sense the motives and the passion behind your employees' actions. And that's what forms a bond, a relationship. If you don't listen carefully and attentively, you'll create a distance between

Discovery Lesson 1

Take a physical or virtual walk through your department and pay close attention to what is going on. Send out a simple message and see what comes back. Listen carefully to the words, and think about what the words really mean, what meaning a certain tone of voice is conveying, and which particular words have the potential to set off or cool down a conflict. If employees speak differently to different co-workers, try to determine the precise difference and what might account for it.

yourself and your employees because you will not hear what they are trying to tell you through more subtle forms of communication.

Applying what you learn from listening to your employees will help you better deliver your messages and ideas to them. By increasing your sensitivity toward your employees, by learning what turns them off and what turns them on, and by identifying the interpersonal dynamics of the members of your staff, you will become keenly aware of the most positive and productive ways to promote communication. Because communication is a two-way street, you need to be sure the "traffic" flows both ways.

Building a Communication Bridge

As a manager, you must create a communication bridge between you and the people who report to you. The purpose of this bridge is for you to connect with each of your employees and for them to connect with you. If you convey the attitude that you care enough about your employees to really listen to them, you can solidify a two-way connection that is mutually rewarding.

Unfortunately, building such a bridge is easier said than done. The problem is that people communicate all the time on three levels: by what they say, by how they say it, and by what they do when they say it. Obviously, in a virtual environment, since you can't see what they do, you need to focus even more on the first two levels.

Let's be clear about what is meant by communication. *Communication* is anything, verbal or nonverbal, that imparts information, thoughts, or feelings. Effective communication between you and your employees occurs when your intended messages and their received messages are essentially the same.

For example, suppose you call an employee's attention to a weakness and then suggest how it can be corrected. If the person receives your message (your constructive criticism) as a gift, your communication is effective. If instead the employee reacts defensively and reads your comment as an attack, your communication is not effective and, therefore, must be modified.

Likewise, for you to accurately receive the intended messages of your employees, you must be a sensitive listener. This means being fully engaged; your brain, ears, eyes, heart, and soul must be involved. You can best accomplish this state by adopting the following attitude: the person communicating to me is the most important person in my life at this moment. That means investing the time, without multitasking, to understand the message you have received and respond thoughtfully.

To genuinely exhibit this attitude, concentrate on the person talking to you, and don't allow yourself to be distracted. Research has shown that our attention spans are shorter than in the past and our distractions have increased; therefore, we must work harder to be attentive listeners. If you don't have time to give an employee your undivided attention, explain the situation and schedule a time when you will be available. It will not do your employee, your organization, or you any good to lend only half an ear.

Detecting Hidden Messages

When listening to employees, bear in mind that most messages have three parts to them, as noted in the previous section.

- The verbal part of the message is revealed by what is actually said or written.
- The emotional part is revealed by how it is said, that is, the tone of voice and the words that are emphasized.
- The nonverbal part is revealed by what is done while it is being said and sometimes afterward. Listen for harmony or dissonance: do the tone of the message and the actions that accompany it reflect the words that were used?

Discovery Lesson 2

Again recall the best manager you ever had. Think back to a time when you came to this manager with a concern that you needed to have resolved. How did this person make you feel during your conversation? What specifically did the manager do to create that feeling? Record your observations in your manager's journal, and keep the lesson as a reminder of what you might do to sharpen your listening skills.

Conversely, think again of the worst manager you ever had, and examine the way this person approached your concerns. Do you find yourself exhibiting any of these characteristics either in person or through messaging? Have you in the past? If so, what steps can you take to change these behaviors? How can you approach issues differently?

See if you can tell what is actually being communicated in the following messages from employees to their managers. The words are clear, but what other messages are there?

- Don't you think we have too many meetings?
- You're in charge; I'll do it the way you want.
- Why is it every time we schedule an appointment it gets canceled?
- What do I have to do to gain some appreciation around here?
- I don't know whether you realize it, but the only time I hear from you is when I screw up in some way.

If you're really listening, you'll hear the hidden message in each of these remarks, as well as others you may encounter daily, and acknowledge them. When you do hear such comments from your employees, ask the speakers what they really mean and if they can suggest some ways to make positive changes. An acknowledgment says, in effect, "I hear what you're really saying, and I invite you to elaborate." Invitation to collaborate in the solutions of any kind, including how to most effectively relay messages and information, establishes productive guidelines for all parties involved.

In response to the first question, for example, you would acknowledge the hidden message by asking if the employee felt there were too many departmental meetings, if he or she felt some of these meetings were unproductive, and what might be done to improve the situation.

Your acknowledgment in turn conveys at least three messages to your employee. First, it recognizes that the employee isn't categorically objecting to the meetings but believes that their content and productivity don't necessitate as many meetings as are actually held. Second, it reflects your understanding that the employee wants to be asked what prompted the comment. And third, it affirms that you care enough about what the employee thinks to ask for his or her opinions on how to make the department more productive.

In the second statement cited—*You're in charge; I'll do it the way you want*—the hidden message may be that the speaker doesn't approve of the method or process of a particular activity. The employee may be too shy to offer his or her opinion and is instead inviting you to solicit it.

By acknowledging the underlying message and asking how the speaker might conduct the process differently, you convey that you are sensitive to the person's thoughts and insights and that you consider the person a valuable member of your department. As you can see, you must be a sensitive listener to decipher underlying emotional messages; you have to hear more than the words.

Let's analyze the remaining three statements on the list to discover what emotional undercurrents reside in them.

Statement: *Why is it every time we make an appointment to get together, the meeting gets canceled?*

Emotional undercurrent: The employee is frustrated and feels undervalued and unimportant. The employee wants your undivided attention and feels entitled to it.

Acknowledgment: Instead of countering with the reasons why you have had to cancel each of your previously scheduled meetings, inform the speaker that you recognize the underlying message. Affirm that the employee is a valuable part of your team and that, in the future, you will strive to keep your appointments without interruptions. Back up this promise with action.

Statement: *What do I have to do to gain some appreciation around here?*

Emotional undercurrent: The speaker feels taken for granted and believes that his or her hard work and successful efforts are not properly credited. Not feeling valued has made the employee angry.

Acknowledgment: State that you do indeed value the person and the person's contributions to your department. Reinforce this statement with private and public commendations of the employee's performance. Ask what actions on your part might make the employee feel more appreciated.

The final statement is a variation of the previous one and carries a similar hidden message: *I don't know whether you realize it, but the only time I hear from you is when I screw up in some way.* Your acknowledgment, likewise, will be a variation of the previous one. Pay attention—catch the employee doing good things.

In summary, acknowledgments of your employees' hidden messages convey your interest in them as people, your sensitivity, and your sincere desire to be the best manager you can be. This attitude will help you find the correct words to acknowledge your employees' emotions. Remember that under no circumstances is it appropriate to judge emotions. If you convey to your employees that their feelings are unwarranted and inappropriate, you will create a negative, divisive atmosphere. Similarly, if you make employees feel insulted, you are likely to precipitate defensive reactions that will negatively affect their productivity and your departmental culture.

You will accomplish three important goals by acknowledging and not judging your employees' emotions. First, your employees will feel that they can trust you and that you care. Second, employees' trust in you will encourage two-way communication. And third, you will assure your employees that they are on a cooperative team.

To underscore the difference between the responses of someone who really listens and one who doesn't, go back to each of the five statements and respond to the verbal part of the message only. By disregarding the underlying messages and responding to only the words, you are announcing that you are insensitive to the speakers' feelings and that you aren't interested in hearing what they really have to say. Obviously, such responses discourage effective communication.

A manager named Mitch shared this anecdote about how responding to only the verbal part of a message proved costly to him. Mitch had an employee, Bill, whom he greatly valued and for whom he would do just about anything to ensure his loyalty. In an effort to do just that, Mitch would ask him at least once a week,

"How are things going, Bill?" Bill, not being much of a talker, would always say, "Fine" or "Very well, thank you."

One week, in response to the same question, Bill said, "OK, I guess." Although this response should have been acknowledged, Mitch wasn't sensitive to the fact that this answer was markedly different from Bill's usual replies. Thus, Mitch assumed that everything was just fine with Bill. After all, that's what the words communicated. You can imagine Mitch's surprise when, after a couple of weeks of this exchange, Bill announced his resignation because he had found another position more to his liking.

A simple acknowledgment—"What do you mean by you 'guess'? Is something wrong?" or "Sounds as if something's bothering you; let's get together to talk about it"—would have given Mitch a chance to resolve Bill's concerns.

Often the emphasis on brevity and speed in the virtual world can preclude such sensitivity. But there can be a significant price to pay.

Principles and Guidelines for Acknowledging Nonverbal Communication

Your employees frequently express their thoughts and feelings by what they do or don't do. Since those nonverbal actions and reactions are often more powerful than words, they must be acknowledged, just as emotions expressed through words must be acknowledged. Under no circumstances should they be ignored. The principles and guidelines that follow, as well as the examples of how to acknowledge both negative and positive actions, will provide you with the tools you need to develop healthy relationships with your employees.

Principle 1: Acknowledge Negative Behavior

Any negative behavior that deviates from a person's normal actions should be acknowledged.

The objectives of this acknowledgment are to determine the causes of the deviation and to solve the problem. An acknowledgment of a negative behavior says, in effect, "I sense that something is not quite right with you, and I'd like to know what it is so we can correct it and move forward."

For example, Anna has been a model employee from the time you hired her. Her disposition is always positive, and her performance has always met your highest standards. However, about a week ago, you noticed a change. She has been short with everyone in the department, and the quality of her work has declined substantially. Essentially, she has not been herself lately. How do you acknowledge what you see?

You might start by pulling Anna aside and telling her that you have noted a change in her behavior. Inform her that this concerns you because she has always been a happy and productive worker, and ask if there is anything she would like to tell you. Make sure the words you choose and your tone of voice are reassuring and nonconfrontational. In so doing you would clearly communicate a caring attitude and a desire to help resolve the problem expressed nonverbally by the employee.

Principle 2: Acknowledge Positive Behavior

Positive behaviors, particularly those that exceed your normal expectations, should also be acknowledged.

Acknowledgments of positive behaviors say, in effect, "I value your work, and I do not take you for granted." The more specific you make the acknowledgment the more effective it will be.

For example, Zack could best be described as a star employee. He typically is the first person in the office and usually stays after normal hours. It's not just a matter of putting in time that makes him valuable to the department but also his attitude toward his responsibilities, which is, in essence, "Good enough is not good enough for me; I want my work to reflect my own high standards and best efforts." Furthermore, he readily volunteers to help co-workers when they have a problem. In all, he is an outstanding asset to the department.

Should those conscientious efforts be taken for granted? Of course not! If you do so, you risk losing a valuable employee. An appropriate acknowledgment of your employee's conscientious contributions to your department would be a simple and effective means of building employee loyalty. An additional acknowledgment might be to take the employee out to lunch or a similar act to show him your appreciation for his contributions above and beyond the call of duty. Saying thank you and expressing your appreciation of employees' efforts will go a long way in building a satisfied and productive workforce.

Principle 3: Be Genuine

Whether you are acknowledging negative or positive nonverbal behavior, the primary attitude that must come through is, "I genuinely care about you as a person as well as in your role as a productive member of our department."

All of us like to feel that we are appreciated for who we are as well as for what we do. We communicate who we are by our physical expressions, physical demeanor, and written communications. But it is not always clear to others what is going on inside. If you sense negative nonverbal behavior, a simple comment such as, "I sense that something is bothering you" or "Seems as if you're having a tough day," is an acknowledgment that might get the employee talking. If, on the other hand, you sense a positive nonverbal behavior, a comment such as, "You look as if you just won the lottery; you want to tell me what's helping you to look and sound so great?" would convey a caring attitude.

In the following situations, the nonverbal messages speak volumes. After you read each setup, apply the guidelines and principles presented in this chapter to answer these questions: (1) What do you hear this employee telling you? (2) How would you effectively acknowledge the nonverbal message?

- Sara is an employee who, until recently, had been performing admirably for as long as you've known her. In the past few days, however, you've noticed a significant decline in both the quality and quantity of her work. Also, during the past two weeks she has been coming in late and leaving exactly when she's supposed to.

- You recently hired Jonah under the assumption that he would fit in with your department. Since his experience was consistent with what you needed, you thought he would require no training to do his job. Now, three weeks after Jonah began work, one of your senior employees calls your attention to the fact that this new employee has been making an inordinate number of errors. Since Jonah hasn't been coming to you for help, you assumed that he knew what he was doing. Except for the errors, there have been no symptoms of other problems.

- Roberto is an employee who is dependable and conscientious in every way, but he is extremely quiet. In departmental meetings, he does not say a word. This bothers you because you know his contributions could benefit the department.

The purpose of the next Discovery Lesson is to increase your confidence in your ability to "listen to behaviors." If you want to be an excellent listener, you must always tune in to all the messages directly conveyed to you as well as those you observe and sense. Verbal, emotional, and behavioral messages all fit together. When any one isn't present, the communication may be incomplete. It's up to you to determine what's missing and then take steps to complete the communication, either by asking questions or by making additional observation.

Throughout your managerial career, keep in mind that every action communicates something. To be an effective manager, you have to make a conscious effort to determine the message communicated by each action.

Remember that you need to hear more than the notes; you need to hear the music.

Discovery Lesson 3

Listed here are a few common emotions or attitudes expressed in work situations. For each one, describe in your manager's journal the nonverbal behaviors you might observe that would indicate these feelings. One or two examples for each are provided to get you started.

- *Fear*: When asked for an opinion on an issue, the employee declines to express it or says, "I don't have an opinion." Fear may also be the cause of employees' reluctance to say what is on their minds.

- *Anger*: An employee raises his or her voice or yells at the slightest provocation. An employee is highly judgmental of other departmental members.

- *Unhappiness*: An employee walks around with a sour face or frequently complains.

continued

- *Boredom or feeling unchallenged*: Procrastination is often a symptom, as is a lack of enthusiasm for assignments.

- *Egotism*: An employee spends too much time texting in a meeting.

- *Conscientiousness*: The employee usually does more than is required. The employee sets high standards, and his or her performance consistently reflects those standards.

- *Caring*: The employee takes a sincere interest in others and asks appropriate questions that reflect this attitude.

- *Respect for fellow employees*: The employee is considerate of people's needs and listens attentively to others.

- *Upbeat and positive in approach to life and work*: The employee has a good sense of humor and looks at the brighter side of life.

Questions to Consider

- *What can you learn by listening to the tone of written messages?*

- *What specifically will you do to improve your listening skills?*

- *What do you anticipate will be the benefits of listening more clearly?*

- *Specifically, how can you promote good listening skills in your department?*

When you're asking questions, view yourself as the student of the person you're questioning.

9

Mastering the Art of Asking Questions

COMMUNICATION, IN TERMS OF BUSINESS, enables people to connect and learn about their respective worlds. Questions are powerful vehicles in communication. They can either strengthen or weaken your connections depending on how they are asked and how they are positioned. That is why it is so important to understand the different types of questions and their purpose. For them to be productive, make sure your questions reflect positive attitudes and honorable intentions. It is not as easy as it sounds. Once we know why we are asking the question, based on our intent, we need to use the right type, with the right tone, at the right time. That will hopefully result in the trust that yields the truth.

Setting the Tone

It's important to set the appropriate tone because the way you form and phrase questions will influence how the responses will be presented. This happens because the questions you ask and how you ask them are emblematic of your thoughts, feelings, and attitudes. They can convey such positive messages as:

"I care about you as a person."
"I'm sincerely interested in your ideas."
"I'd like to know so that I can help you solve your problems."
"I'd like to understand you better."
"I need specific information from you."
"I want to help."
"I want to stimulate you to think."
"I want to stimulate a discussion."

Even a manager with the best intentions may ask questions in a way that places employees on the defensive. For example, such questions as "Why do you have such a bad attitude?" or "How many times have I told you not to do that?" are not really questions. They are actually adverse judgmental statements in the form of questions. In these examples, the questioner is not really interested in an answer; the true objective is to chastise or indict the person being addressed.

When you ask the right questions in the right ways, you can learn much from your employees. You can find out what's happening and why. You can gain valuable information and insights to help you function better in your job. You can also learn about what your employees are thinking, what turns them on, what turns them off, what upsets them, what stimulates them, and more.

In your role as manager, a primary task is to get your staff to contribute and participate. Communication is a two-way road.

Before you can accurately direct your staff, you must understand the people you are directing, and you do that by asking. It takes a few additional minutes out of your busy day, but it will save a great deal of time over the long haul.

Have a Clear Destination

Fundamental to the art of asking the right questions is knowing exactly what you are looking for. When you have a firm idea of what you need, write it down. This gives you a focus and destination, analogous to your preparation before taking a road trip. If you've planned the journey and you know your destination, you'll get there. Even if you have to take a detour, you will get to where you want to go. Without a clear-cut destination, you can drive for a long time and use a lot of fuel but not end up in the place you really want to be. It may be fun to do that, and it can be an interesting diversion, but it won't accomplish your intended mission.

You can always make time for fun if you want to, but the purpose of this chapter is to help you stay on track and reach your goals. Those goals must be apparent to all parties, and your staff will follow your lead. Unless you're simply making small talk, when you're asking your employees business-related questions, have a definite destination in mind. Don't allow yourself to stray from your course.

You may be thinking, "Everyone asks questions all the time. What's new here?" Although it's true that people habitually ask questions, often those questions are posed with no plan and without forethought to the reaction they might elicit. Here's a simple example of how the question determines the answer: If you ask someone to describe the biggest problems he or she faces at work, you'll get a list of problems. If, on the other hand, you ask about that person's greatest opportunities, you will get a much different listing. You get what you ask for, so be careful how you ask.

As further illustration, the following scene was played out recently in a department store:

A woman and her young daughter, probably eight or nine years old, were shopping for a dress for the child. The mother gestured to a rack of dresses and asked, "Which dress do you want?"

The little girl smiled and pointed to her choice. "This one."

"Oh, that wouldn't look good on you," said the mother. "The color and style are all wrong for you."

"But I like it. I think it's nice."

The mother picked up another dress. "How about this one?"

"I don't like that one. I like the one I picked out."

In the end, the little girl was in tears, her mother was angry with her, and no dress was purchased that day.

What went wrong? The mother asked the wrong question. She asked her daughter to make a selection from a wide variety of choices. The mother established a broad, unrestricted range despite the fact that she had already imposed certain limitations herself regarding color and style. She asked a question, and she prompted the child to make a selection. When the child complied, the mother rejected her decision.

There probably would have been little turmoil if the mother had established a different sequence of events. Since she knew what her acceptable range of choices included, she could have selected three or four dresses that met her criteria and then asked, "Which one of these pretty dresses would you like?"

Whichever of those dresses the little girl picked would have been acceptable to the mother, and the daughter would have been happy with her choice. It was her decision, after all. The mother also would have been happy because she had provided guidance and direction. It would have been one of those win-win situations rather than a disaster, because the framing of the question often dictates the outcome.

Match the Question to the Need

You have a variety of methods at your disposal to gather and exchange information. The following sections outline five techniques for results-oriented communication: closed questions, open questions, probing questions, echoes, and follow-up questions.

Closed Questions

Closed questions are useful when you want to confirm information or when you want a straightforward answer, with no elaboration, to a straightforward question. These kinds of questions do not engender discussion. Furthermore, they might even hinder a free exchange of information because they often seem to be an interrogation.

Closed questions produce short, usually one-word answers and do not leave much room for discussion. This category includes queries that begin with "Can," "Do," "Is," "Will," "When," "Who," and "Did." Note the ways such closed questions can be answered:

Question Beginning with	Typical Answer
Can	Yes or No
Do	Yes or No
Is	Yes or No
Will	Yes, No, or Maybe
When	Tuesday
Who	Charlie
Did	Yes or No

Frequently, simple answers such as these are not satisfactory if you are looking for explanations, reasons, and examples. If you are asking a question to get information, the person of whom you're asking the question must be persuaded or encouraged to share that information. Closed questions will yield only minimum information. To gain more information, you must get your employee to talk more than you. You increase your chances of accomplishing that by employing open questions.

Open Questions

Open questions usually start with "How," "What," and "Why." These formats require lengthier responses than closed questions. These require extra attention to the attitude, intent, and tone of the question. Make sure questions intended for resolving curiosity are exactly that and not used for building a case or a trap.

Crafting open questions requires more attention than phrasing closed questions. Once you say the first word, you have to figure out what the rest of the sentence will be. You have to identify your area of interest and focus. You might begin questions with the following:

"How will . . . ?"
"What . . . ?"
"Why . . . ?"

Tread carefully with such questions because, as has been demonstrated, the way you ask them will usually preprogram the answer. It will stake out the territory for exploration, and your employee will follow your lead. For example, if you were to ask someone, "What is the toughest challenge you have to overcome?" it's logical for the person to tell you how he or she views the challenge and plans to deal with it. Then again, if you were to ask, "What do you need from me to meet your current challenge?" you may find yourself more involved in this person's caseload than you care to be. Open questions can be valuable; just remember to construct them so that you ask for what you really want to know.

"Why" questions are especially tricky. While they are as legitimate as others, you have to be particularly cognizant of how they might be perceived by your employee. This form of question can do much more than ask for reasons. It can be interpreted as a request for information or as accusatory and entrapping. For example, here is a "why" question that, clearly, simply seeks information: "I was wondering, why did you choose option X rather than Y?" It may, however, sound judgmental, implying, "Why would you do such a foolish thing?"

Don't ask "why" when there is nothing the responder could say that would be acceptable to you. Those are trap questions, which place the person on the defensive. For example: "Why did you submit this sloppy report?" or "Why did you buy such an ugly tie?" No answer to either of those shots would satisfy the questioner. There is no way the responder can win or can infer that the questioner really wants information. Such questions are obviously accusatory. Here again, you can see how the framing of the question determines the answer.

Probing Questions

Probing questions dig more deeply into an area already established by either a closed or an open question. They prod responders to talk about what is important to them. The objective of using probes is to obtain additional detail about the subject being presented to you. When you use either an open or a closed question, it is you who identifies the area for discussion. An appropriate question of either type will prime the pump; information will start to flow, but it might stop abruptly. There is an easy way to keep it flowing, and you don't have to work hard to think up new questions. All you have to do is call on a short list of standards that will fit almost any situation. Try these:

"What gives you that impression?"
"Can you help me understand . . . ?"
"What makes you say that?"

"Really?"

"Would you elaborate?"

"Would you give me an example?"

"What else should I know?"

"Why do you say that?"

"Tell me more."

This format can fit any situation, regardless of the topic. Probes such as these keep the conversation moving. Moreover, the responders are invited to select the areas that are important to them. As you hear what aspect responders select and what they add, you develop greater insight into what is important to them. In fact, people who are adept at using these techniques are regarded as great conversationalists because they can keep others talking.

You'll have many occasions to use probes in your managerial career. For instance, suppose you are interviewing someone for a job. In response to one of your questions, the applicant says, "I have good communication skills." You might probe by asking, "What kind of communication skills are you referring to?" Or, if an employee says, "I'm having trouble with Frankie," you might ask, "Will you elaborate?" The benefit is that you quickly find out what you need to know without working hard.

Echoes

Probes can also take the form of an echo, a technique in which you repeat a few of the responder's words back to the person. In almost every instance, the responder will keep talking. It's that simple.

Suppose a person says, "I'm having a tough time with this assignment." You respond, "A tough time?" Or, a disgruntled employee says, "It's unfair that I get blamed for everything that goes wrong around here." Your echo might be, "Everything?" or "Get blamed?" The echo says in effect, "I heard you, and you are invited to continue telling me whatever you want to tell me."

Echoes are a handy tool for probing when a person talks in generalizations or abstractions. Try it the next time someone falls back on a generalization when talking to you. All you have to do is echo, "Always?" or "Never?" See how it works in response to generalizations such as "John's attitude is terrible" or "Mary is so irresponsible." Just say, "Terrible?" or "Irresponsible?" You'll probably get more information than you ever expected. Another reliable alternative is to reply, "Tell me more." Then stand back because the new information will come in waves.

Follow-Up Questions

This last technique is a variation of the first three, but it is used to gather data, evidence, and support of an initial comment. Here, you are following up on something the person said to round out your information on the subject in which you're interested. For example, "Earlier you said, _____ . I'd like to discuss this in a little more detail."

That sentence, "Earlier you said, _____ ," does something else for you and your staff: it demonstrates that you listened. When you communicate that to your staff, you also demonstrate that you value them; you value what they have to say, and you want them to tell you more.

This harks back to the chapter on the value of listening. Once you ask a question, be ready to be an active listener. Here is a guiding rule: If you don't plan to listen to the answer, don't ask the question! You'll just be wasting everyone's time.

Match Your Delivery to Your Questions

All of the five major questioning techniques described are useful, as long as the person with whom you're talking interprets what you say as you intended. That is where the art comes in. The message they receive from the question you ask is dependent on your attitude, body language, and framing of the question. These are all easier if you think in the back of your mind, "The person I am speaking to right now is the most important person in my world." It sounds crazy, but watch how it changes how you listen and respond.

Make sure your body language does not contradict your question. If you start with "I am interested, so can you tell me about . . . ?" be sure you are not doing something else that makes you look uninterested. Some tips on body language may differ depending on the culture, but some are universal.

One suggestion is to make eye contact both when you talk and when you listen. When you look at your employees, it demonstrates that you value them. A second suggestion would be to take notes. It is often appropriate to record key points of your talks with staff members. Again, when you write down people's words, you demonstrate that you value the comments—and the speaker. Be sure to accompany your note taking with an explanation such as "That's important" or "I didn't know that." Thoughtful, responsive note taking is respectful and when done well can serve as fodder for follow-up questions and conversations.

Confirm, Clarify, or Expand

Asking the right questions in the right ways will put you in close touch with your employees. The right way will depend on your intentions, so be sure of what you want to do: do you want to confirm, clarify, or expand?

When you want to confirm information, closed questions might be your best choice because you'll generally get "yes" or "no" responses. You'll get the short answers that can lead you to specific action or agreement.

When you want to clarify, the open question will produce the details you need to fully understand the response. Open questions enable you to seek additional data in areas you feel are important.

When you want to expand, use the probes, echoes, and follow-up questions that allow and encourage answers that reflect the responder's interests and priorities. Once you identify what is important to the person, follow that lead and the person will keep talking.

Use these five techniques when you're asking questions. Know what you want, and choose the course that will lead you to your destination. Know exactly where you want to go and what you want to learn.

When you're asking questions, view yourself as the student of the person you're questioning. And remember, you don't learn much when you are talking. That means, when you ask questions, silence is golden. Listen—really listen. Remember also that there's a good reason we each have two ears but only one mouth. Listen more than you talk when you want to gather information. If we talk too much, we might set up barriers and not get what we want. Good communication keeps the traffic flowing in both directions.

Practice, Practice, Practice

Asking the right questions in the right ways does not come naturally to most of us. To become comfortable with these techniques, practice them whenever you talk with your neighbors, your family, or your spouse. Practice them with everyone. Don't wait to use the questioning techniques until you are face-to-face with a recalcitrant staff member. You can practice on any service person at a restaurant or store.

Just as with any sport you might play, you practice the skills over and over before you get into a game. That way, in the pressure of competition, you will use the skills automatically. You won't have to think your way through a behavior if you have made it a natural part of yourself. So, practice, practice, and practice some more on your children, in social settings, anytime you have the opening.

You don't have to juggle all of the techniques right away or at the same time. Pick one or two that feel comfortable and work with only them until you can easily see their application and the results they can produce, and then try the others. Soon you'll be using all of them with regularity, and you'll be pleased with what you accomplish.

Discovery Lesson 1

Try out some or all of the five questioning techniques the next time you're at a dinner party. Listen first and decide what your purpose for your question is so you choose the right one. Then make sure you are tuned in to the response so that you can continue if need be.

By using the techniques you've learned, you will involve others in the conversation. You'll be impressed by how easily the conversations unfold and what you might discover.

Discovery Lesson 2

Listen to other people's questions. Try to figure out what types of questions they are asking and see if they are getting the intended results.

Once you've developed the skill of asking the right questions in the right ways, you'll be surprised by how much you will learn and grow professionally—and personally. When you practice and hone these questioning skills, you become an accomplished conversationalist, lauded in a variety of situations. When you demonstrate interest in others, they will open up to you. When you demonstrate that you value people's ideas, they will share them with you. And when your staff members share their ideas, you have more data with which to make your management decisions.

These are basic techniques that you can modify once you have mastered them. Imprint your own style, of course, but use them, and see what happens.

Questions to Consider

- *What do I need to know about my employees and how should I ask the questions?*

- *How can I better align my questions with what I need to know?*

- *When I am asking questions, how can I convey a positive intent?*

If you treat your friends as if they are enemies, someday you won't be able to tell the difference.

10

Eliminating Weeds from Your Departmental Garden

THE SINGLE TOUGHEST CHALLENGE OF gardeners is to make sure weeds don't invade or take over their garden. Unfortunately, weeds grow faster than desired plants and they rob gardens of vital nutrients. They detract from a garden's beauty and they require time, money, and energy to eradicate. These are the same time, money, and energy that are needed to promote the growth of your healthy garden. Furthermore, if weeds are allowed to proliferate, they can destroy a previously thriving garden. So, you need to catch them early.

In applying this analogy to your departmental culture, keep in mind this definition: "A weed is a valueless, troublesome, or noxious plant growing wild, especially one that grows profusely or on cultivated ground to the exclusion or injury of the desired crop."

In business, weeds are not people but attitudes, behaviors, and actions, either yours or your employees', that are toxic to your departmental garden. It is your job to recognize them and remove them quickly, consistently, and systematically. When many weeds come from the same source, you might need to remove the source.

Identifying Departmental Weeds

Departmental weeds take a variety of forms; some are easy to identify and some are less obvious. Nevertheless, the key to removing them is learning to recognize them. Again, weeds are attitudes, behaviors, and actions that are:

- Not aligned with your departmental objectives and problem-solving culture
- Nonproductive and prevent the betterment of your department
- Noncollaborative and promote "siloed thinking" within your workgroup

Following are descriptions of the most toxic weeds. To best understand them, read each description and reflect on specific examples that exemplify these weeds in your own department.

- **Defensiveness.** Defensiveness of any sort is potentially the single most pernicious weed. It usually grows from fear or insecurity. Examples of defensive behavior are blaming, finding fault, close-mindedness, and making excuses; such actions sabotage the problem-solving process. When people are defensive, they act irresponsibly and emotionally. As a consequence, projects or tasks get stalled or not completed to your level of satisfaction. Defensiveness derails productivity.

- **Negativism.** Negativism, a byproduct of defensiveness, feeds on itself. It quickly demoralizes and deteriorates the culture if it's allowed to flourish. By example, if you say to an employee, or one employee says to another, "This won't work!" or "That's a bad idea!" or "This task/job/meeting is stupid!" the ball starts rolling. Once it starts, people take the opportunity to jump in and vent their issues too. That's when negativity starts to grow. It has the power to cloud employees' positive outlooks, inhibit creativity, discourage collaboration, and stifle productive exchange.

- **Labeling.** Any time someone uses general statements to describe a person or a work product, they are labeling. For example, an employee complains that a co-worker is ineffective, or irresponsible, or sloppy, or rude. These negative labels don't say anything meaningful about the person or situation in question. And they don't identify the specific *problem*. They are just unproductive expressions of their anger and frustration. With the increase of a diverse and global workforce and differences in approach, people resort to labeling in lieu of learning, understanding, and adapting.

- **Distrust.** Distrust dissolves your departmental foundation. Whether your employees do not trust you, you do not trust them, or they do not trust each other, lack of trust is very damaging to your success as a manager.

Following are some ways you may inadvertently demonstrate distrust. If you micromanage, you demonstrate lack of trust in your staff and in your abilities as a manager. If you do not delegate work when appropriate, they may think you don't trust them to do the work. If you don't elicit honest, productive feedback from your employees, they will think you are trying to hide from something.

Perceived distrust yields untrustworthiness. It is a vicious circle. Distrust discourages risk taking and initiative in your employees, and then you can't trust them to be productive members of your team. All of this undermines the cohesiveness of your department if it is allowed to proliferate.

- **Lack of accountability.** You will fail your department if you refuse to take responsibility for issues that arise. Likewise, your employees should accept responsibility for their actions. Before a problem can be solved, someone has to own it and then ensure that a course of action will be taken to rectify the situation. Passing the buck will not accomplish anything and will lead to an infinite, costly circle of blame.

- **Impatience.** People also have varying abilities and aptitudes; it is unfair and unreasonable to assume that everyone has the same potential, can excel in the same manner, and can work at the same pace. Expressing impatience only worsens the situation.

  Impatience can be expressed in many ways. You or your employees may expect more from someone than the person is capable of giving and become frustrated and impatient with the person. Or you may expect too much too soon and give up on the struggling employee prematurely. As is the case with some plants, certain people require more time to develop or grow and thus require more of your patience in order to fulfill their potential. Not giving them that stunts their growth.

Now that you know how to identify them, you're ready to learn how to keep weeds from taking root in your department. This is the topic of the next section.

Prevent Weeds from Taking Root

Just as gardens have weeds that impact their foundation, production, and yield, so do organizations. Organizational weeds, however, adversely affect profits, morale, and productivity in your department. As a manager within your organization, you have the power to prevent weeds from infiltrating your turf. That's a power you must exercise in order to fulfill your mission of creating a profitable, productive department staffed by people with positive attitudes.

Of course, weeds, by their very nature, crop up uninvited and without warning. But you can prevent them from taking root and proliferating by creating a problem-solving approach to disagreements and differences of opinion. Learning how to do this will be well worth your time and effort. Below are some responses that will help you "kill the weeds." These are general approaches used to disengage the emotion and should be customized for your specific situations.

- Respond to any weed statement with, "I am sorry you feel that way" or "Thank you for sharing" or "I did not see it that way."
- Respond to any weed behavior with a statement of fact: "That is not how we do things here" or questions like "I am not sure how that contributes to our goals and objectives. Can you explain?"

- Respond to any other weed by taking ownership yourself for finding a solution. Excuses or someone to blame provides fertile ground for weeds to grow. Removing excuses or power from a weedy situation is a step toward eliminating the source.

In a weed-infested culture, decisions are reactive: based on fear, adverse judgments, personal opinions, and limiting beliefs about how things have to be. However, in a culture that's reasonably weed-free, ideas flourish, productivity is high, quality performance is a source of pride, and collaboration delivers innovative solutions.

These enticing benefits should spur you to create such a culture. Therefore, pay attention and recognize weeds when you see them, prevent them from spreading, and discourage new ones from growing.

Building a Weed-Free Department

When you accepted the responsibility of departmental manager, you made certain implied promises that you must now fulfill. The most important implied promise was to create a culture in which each employee has an opportunity to realize his or her potential. That opportunity grows out of meaningful challenges, a cooperative and positive atmosphere, encouragement and appropriate direction from you, and freedom from negative forces—or weeds—that can interfere with employees' effectiveness.

Creating a totally weed-free departmental culture is idealistic and, therefore, impossible. People are imperfect and often are influenced by their nonrational emotions. Nevertheless, you can strive to create a culture similar to the one that your own "best manager" developed.

The process begins with a statement to the department expressing your desire and asking for each employee's help to achieve it. Using your own words, the message you want to get across is essentially this:

> In addition to the departmental mission, which is expressed in our mission statement, I, as manager of the department, have my own private mission. It is to create an environment in which all employees feel motivated to perform their respective jobs to the best of their abilities and are encouraged to act responsibly toward one another. To ensure that both of these objectives are fulfilled, distractions, which are like weeds in a garden, must be reduced to a minimum.

Clarify for your employees that "weeds" are attitudes, behaviors, and/or actions, either yours or your employees', that are toxic and do not serve the best interests of the department and its members. You can refer to the various characteristics of a weed presented earlier in the chapter, and you may even want to distribute copies of the description so that employees can have it readily available as a reminder. (See the Appendix for reproducible text.)

The final step in reducing the opportunities for weeds to enter your departmental garden is requesting that employees take responsibility for being problem solvers and avoiding negative, weedlike behaviors. If every person in the department, including you, makes a conscious effort to create a positive, fertile working environment that's free of weeds, then everyone will benefit.

In addition to expressing this message to your current employees, when you hire new people, make sure they are problem solvers and not prone to defensiveness. Although you can never be 100 percent sure of hiring people who are free of weedlike inclinations, you can increase your chances by listening carefully to their responses to your questions. In particular, listen to their descriptions of how they handle adversity. Telltale signs include shifting blame, finding fault, making excuses, and failing to take responsibility for mistakes.

During your interviews with prospective employees, you may also want to tell them that your private mission is to create an environment in which all employees feel motivated to perform to the best of their abilities and are encouraged to act responsibly toward one another. Then ask candidates how they can contribute to the fulfillment of this mission. If you get a favorable response, you're probably looking at someone who would be a healthy addition to that environment.

How to Deal with Stubborn Weeds

Creating an open and productive working environment is an ambitious undertaking. While conscientious employees will embrace this fresh outlook, others will stubbornly resist it. They may be mired in their old habits of blaming and finding fault with others, bullying fellow employees, and allowing their egos to dictate their actions. Since these actions are harmful to your department, it is imperative that you put a stop to them.

To help you discourage people who insist on generating weeds, you might want to enlist the aid of other members of your department. The more people you involve in a cause, the more successful it will be. You may find that the merits extend beyond your department to the whole organization. Wouldn't that be a nice benefit?

If all your positive efforts fail with someone you're certain is a weed producer, and you've put the person on notice, you have only one resort: uproot the weed. It is better to remove a weed than to allow it to ruin your garden.

Discovery Lesson

There are weeds that come up in your conversations, messages, and behaviors around your department. Note them in your manager's journal for a week. Review the six "weed" types detailed in the preceding section, and try to match each weed to a type.

The purpose of this activity is not to dwell on negative behaviors but to be able to identify them when they arise. The more adept you are at recognizing them, the better you will become at resolving them.

Questions to Consider

- *What are some examples of weedlike behaviors in my department?*

- *How will I promote my personal mission to be adopted by all team members?*

- *How else can I deflect unwanted weeds from invading my departmental garden?*

- *Given that many interactions take place through technology, what productive templates can I create to discourage "weed-inspired" communication?*

Criticism is a valuable gift. But, to be viewed as such, it must be properly wrapped and sensitively presented.

It is kinder to be gently direct than to be cruelly silent.

11

Giving the Gift of Constructive Criticism

A MAJOR SUCCESS FACTOR FOR you as manager is increasing your ability to improve the quality and effectiveness of the people under your influence. Constructive criticism can help. When delivered with appropriate intent and timing, it is the kindest, most generous way of saying, "Since you matter to me, I want you to be the best you can be. My criticisms are gifts that will help you achieve your objectives."

As nice as that sounds in theory, what would you do if an employee exercised poor judgment in handling a problem? What would you do if an employee failed to meet your expectations? What would you do if you were disappointed with an employee who did not fulfill a promise? These are serious issues. How do you correct an employee without being offensive? How do you criticize without being critical? How do you confront without being confrontational?

The hard truth is that when an employee does something that is harmful to your department's culture, or does something you know is wrong, you must let the person know. In such cases, you have the specific obligation to tell your employees what they did wrong, explain why the action disappointed you, provide whatever help they need to correct the situation, and make sure they understand what they can do to prevent a recurrence. The secret is in the ability to deliver the message clearly, but package it as a gift. Achieving that is the subject of this chapter.

Change Begins with Awareness

Put yourself in the employee's shoes for a moment: Imagine you are an employee who inadvertently has not fulfilled several of your manager's expectations, or who exercised poor judgment in handling a customer complaint, or who did something else that is unacceptable to your manager. How would you want your manager to address the situation? Here are four possible responses:

- Ignore your actions so as not to hurt your feelings.
- Chastise you, either privately or in front of your colleagues, and make you feel guilty or stupid.
- Tell you what you did wrong but offer no suggestions for improving.
- Call your attention to what you did or didn't do that was unacceptable, determine the cause of your misdemeanor,

agree on a course of corrective action, and discuss what needs to be done to prevent the problem from recurring.

Clearly, the last reaction is what you would expect of a professional manager. This tactic is both effective and benevolent. It is effective in that the manager confronts you with your errors rather than allowing you to believe that everything is fine. It is benevolent because it involves you in the solution to a problem of your own making. That is a thoughtful gift, don't you agree?

This type of feedback is what your employees should expect from you. They trust you to tell them how they can improve their performance. They also trust you not to collect bricks or to build invisible walls. In short, they trust you to be forthright and supportive and to do everything in your power to help them succeed.

If you do not fairly criticize or confront employees when it's appropriate, you are setting them up to fail. How can people improve if they're unaware that they did something wrong? Awareness is the beginning of change. As their manager, you must make your employees aware of their shortcomings and mistakes and provide them with the guidance they need to improve and correct their errors. You don't deprive them of gifts that can make them better employees and people.

Although helpful criticism is a valuable gift, many managers lack the courage to offer it because they confuse criticism with adverse judgments.

Differentiating Between Gifts and Adverse Judgment

It's not criticism or feedback itself but the way it is offered that separates thoughtful criticism from adverse judgments. When a manager provides feedback with the attitude of "These are gifts for people I regard highly as an aid in their development" and assumes his or her employees are grateful, you can be certain that those views and assumptions will prove to be a self-fulfilling prophecy. But, being a positive prophecy, the "gifts" would be properly wrapped, sensitively presented, and, therefore, gratefully received.

Adverse judgments, on the other hand, are statements that chastise and, either intentionally or unintentionally, make the person being judged feel bad and prompt defensiveness. Typically, adverse judgments begin with "you" and are followed by negative comments.

This is what an adverse judgment would sound like: "You didn't fulfill your promise to me. How could you be so irresponsible? You really let me down by not doing what you were supposed to when you were supposed to do it."

As a professional manager, you must convince yourself that warranted criticism can benefit your employees. You must believe that your employees trust you to give them gifts of criticism. They trust you because deep within, they know your intentions are honorable. You must also assume that when you fail to criticize employees when it is warranted, you are inadvertently sabotaging them. Finally, you must be less concerned with your feelings about criticizing than in doing the right thing in the right way for the sake of your employees.

How to Present Your Gifts Properly

Intended to be helpful and solve problems, criticism should accomplish three objectives:

1. Help the receiver become aware of what you see and why it's a problem
2. Show the receiver what changes will alleviate the problem
3. Increase the likelihood that the behavior won't recur

To achieve those objectives, you need the cooperation of the other party. You will likely gain employees' cooperation if you treat them as friends and if you follow certain guidelines.

First, make sure your criticism identifies the specific problem that concerns you. For example, suppose an employee submits a report to you that's riddled with spelling errors. Your criticism might be, "It bothers me to receive a report that's filled with spelling mistakes." Or suppose an employee is demanding of the department secretary. You might say, "I believe in treating every member of the department with respect. That's why it bothers me when you make demands of our secretary."

Second, make sure you tell the employee what specifically you want that would resolve your problem. Concerning the error-filled report, you could say, "Your reports would look more professional if you used the spell check that's available to you" or "Before handing in a report to me, please make sure there are no spelling errors." In the example of the demanding employee, you could say, "When making a request of our secretary, ask for what you need, rather than tell her, in a demanding voice, what you want. As my grandmother used to say, 'You can catch more flies with honey than with vinegar.'"

Third, make sure you agree on how to prevent the problem from recurring. (This guideline is flexible and may not always be applicable.) For example, "Could we agree that you will proofread your reports before you give them to me?" or "Could we agree that any expenditure above x dollars will be checked with me?"

To help you incorporate constructive criticism as a teaching tool, adopt the following attitudes:

- Criticisms are gifts my team members deserve. It's my responsibility as a manager to provide them.
- When delivering my gift it should include what specifically I want, need, or expect, without adversely judging anyone as a prelude to the request.
- Never criticize emotions, since emotions are neither right nor wrong.
- Only criticize behavior, never the person.
- It is kinder to be gently direct than cruelly silent.

How to Gain Cooperation from Other Managers Without Being Critical

There will be times when you need the cooperation of other managers but are not getting it. Usually, these managers will tell you they are too busy and can't spare the time. Although you may be angry and be tempted to criticize (actually, adversely judge) them, or to give them a piece of your mind, that's not a good idea. Doing so would likely spoil your chances of getting what you want or need from them.

In such cases, criticism is inappropriate. So, resist the temptation of criticizing noncooperative fellow managers. Keep your eyes on your objective, which is to obtain what you need from them. Make it easy for them to give you what you want. Don't hand them an excuse to reject you.

An approach that has been successful follows these steps: engage, acknowledge, present, request. *Engage* them in a discussion. *Acknowledge* their limitations. *Present* your need. *Request* their assistance. This is how it works:

Ask the manager whose help you need to give you a few minutes to discuss an issue. Most people won't deny you that. Then, when you meet, say something to this effect: "Like you, my staff and I want to do the best job we know how. To achieve that objective, we need your help. I know your department is busy, just as we are, but without your cooperation, we're going to fall short of what we need to accomplish. What can I say or do to gain your department's cooperation?"

By all means, use your own words. However you phrase it, make your request positive. Never make your counterpart feel that he or she hasn't been cooperative.

Discovery Lesson

In your manager's journal, describe expectations that were unfulfilled by three people who work for you.

Now pretend you want to deliver feedback to each of these employees regarding the respective behavior. For each unfulfilled expectation, take two approaches:

- Be a friend, and criticize constructively; present the person you're criticizing with a well-packaged, attractively wrapped, and useful gift.

- Adversely judge the action, not the person.

continued

Example: Remember that criticisms are helpful gifts. Let's say an employee promised to submit a report. The due date arrives, and no report is forthcoming. When you go to your employee to request it, she says she hasn't got it but she'll get it to you in a few days. You must inform her that this behavior is unacceptable. At the same time, you want her to know what acceptable behavior is.

This is what the criticism might sound like: "I am not sure what happened, but when I ask for something on a specific day and you promise to deliver it, I need it on that day. Next time, if you see that you can't deliver what you promised, please tell me in advance so I can work around the change. Is that a reasonable request?"

After completing this Discovery Lesson, reflect on what you learned and record your insights in your journal.

Questions to Consider

- *How can you deliver feedback as a gift versus an adverse judgment?*

- *What can you request from another manager using the new approach?*

- *It's easy to confuse helpful criticism with lecturing to a person whose behavior needs correction. What's the difference between the two?*

PART III

Building on Your Foundation

Creating a solid departmental foundation is a good start toward fulfilling your responsibilities as a professional manager. But it is only a start. Now that you have learned how to lay the groundwork for a positive, productive department consisting of staff members who are engaged, eager to take risks, and work well together, you need to learn how to successfully build on that foundation.

In this part, you will learn how to hire "value-adding" people to your department. Your department's effectiveness depends on the quality of the people who compose it. With sound preparation and practice, you can recruit personnel who are ready, willing, and able to help drive your department to new levels of achievement.

You will learn how to conduct performance reviews that benefit your employees. Performance reviews, when done right, help employees improve their skills and develop qualities that will make them more effective.

You will learn how to plan and conduct productive departmental meetings. Departmental meetings can easily become a waste of time. Or they can be useful and productive gatherings. Everyone involved will benefit from these meetings once you know what specifically you need to do to make them more productive.

You will find out how to make it safe for your staff to take reasonable risks. As a manager, you must encourage your employees to expand their comfort zones. If you don't, you stymie their contributions to your department. You must also teach them how to assess which risks are reasonable and which ones should not be taken.

You will discover how to delegate effectively. With rapidly increasing demands, knowing how to share work with employees is essential. But, as with everything else you do as a manager, you must delegate correctly, in the proper terms and with the proper attitude, and to the right people. Knowing how to evaluate that is crucial for success.

You'll develop mastery for resolving conflicts. Differences in perceptions and opinions often create tension. No matter how solid your departmental foundation, conflicts will seep through. As long as the resolutions lead to greater mutual understanding and win-win outcomes, they can actually strengthen your department.

You will learn how to deal with and prevent harassment. Sexual harassment is not the only type that plagues companies.

Regardless of the nature of the harassment you encounter, you must know how to prevent it from harming your work environment and your employees.

By applying the knowledge you gain from these chapters, with insights and approaches learned earlier, you will accomplish two important objectives:

- You will perpetuate a problem-solving department, built with employees who are productive and encouraged to grow.
- You will provide a model for them to build on in their future supervisory or managerial positions.

Let's move forward.

As a manager, you are only as good as the people under your influence. Hire the best and treat them well to reap the most benefits from your employees.

12

Hiring the Right People

WITHOUT A GOOD TEAM OF EMPLOYEES to help you carry out your responsibilities, you're at risk of not fulfilling your ambition to be a successful, professional manager. Just as a good gardener must pick the right seeds and soil and create the right conditions, you must pick the right people and create the conditions for them to grow.

Identifying the right people for your department depends on what you want to accomplish and what kind of work you are doing. For any position you want to fill, you must first clearly define the job requirements for yourself. Only after you have a firm concept of what a particular job is about can you select the best person for it. This is an expertise that you must develop.

Hone Your Skills Before You Need Them

Hiring the best person for a job starts by delineating exactly what the person must be able to do to perform the job most efficiently and effectively. The best way to know what you are looking for is to write down exactly what you expect of the person who will fill the position, because you can't fool the discipline of facing a blank piece of paper. To see for yourself the value of writing down your expectations, complete the following exercise in your manager's journal.

Hiring staff is typically a significant part of a manager's responsibility, and with every hire, you must do it right the first time in order to gain optimum productivity. If you make a bad hire, the person probably won't last very long on the job, and you'll have to go through the process all over again. This is a poor use of time and is expensive to boot.

According to the U.S. Department of Labor, "A bad hire will cost a company the equivalent of that employee's salary for a six-month period." It certainly won't take very many of these to have a serious impact on your bottom line. A bad hire can be a substantial mistake, but it's one you can avoid by using your professional skills. Try the suggested exercise with a few people in your department now. Don't wait until there is a vacant position. This allows you to practice first and perform later. Your strategy is to hone your skills before you need them in an actual situation.

Again, be specific about what you want to accomplish, and then practice, practice, practice. Too many managers shoot from the hip or act on instinct. If you do either of these, you might be lucky and make a good hiring decision, but it's more likely you'll make an expensive error.

Discovery Lesson 1

Pick a position within your department and write down the job skills and knowledge that you think are required to do this job well. Then ask people in the department who occupy a similar position what skills and knowledge they need to do their jobs well. Since they are so close to the real task, they can tell you exactly what it requires. Be careful not to include how they need to get it done, unless the skills are absolutely required. Check your list of what you thought against the list of requirements identified by the workers, and modify your list if necessary. Working from this detailed description of the job requirements, compose several questions that would be appropriate to ask applicants to determine if they possess the identified skills and qualities needed to succeed in this job.

This might seem like a lot of busywork, but this discipline could save you considerable difficulty, and money, in the long run. With more competition in the job market it is even more important to know what you need in a new hire. We've all heard that time is money, but many managers don't heed the implications of that expression. It sounds good, but often it doesn't change any behavior. As a new manager, you should pay especially close attention to how you use your time and the time of your employees.

Basic Steps to Good Hiring

Armed with a detailed, clear synopsis of what is required of a candidate to fill a specified position, you're ready to proceed, with care, to the next step.

Announcing the Job

Companies must comply with a host of laws, rules, and regulations regarding the posting of job vacancies in order to provide equal employment opportunities. Talk with your human resources staff to get their input on the appropriate procedures for your company and department. The best advice is to know the law and, if you don't know, ask.

Several avenues are open to you for identifying and selecting the best candidate for a position. You may announce the position through whatever forms are appropriate for your company, association, or profession.

Perhaps someone in your department or elsewhere in your organization is interested in the job. Because managers work closely with their employees, they often see those employees in a specific role and assume they wouldn't be interested in a different position. This can be a costly oversight. Managers sometimes just don't think about their staffs' career paths or encourage employees to move up or on to another position. This is how good talent gets lost, so be sure to inform employees of upcoming opportunities, and be supportive of their efforts to grow. That will be good for them, for you, and for the organization.

Screening Applicants

When the job posting is distributed, you'll probably get plenty of applications and résumés. They are your primary sources of information about the candidates' work experience, abilities, and skills. When you review the submissions, write down what you have learned about the candidates and what specific actions they have accomplished. Many résumés contain an extraordinary amount of information, some of which you don't need or want, so list only the facts that relate to the abilities you're looking for in the ideal candidate. As a final step, you can research them online to see if they have a Web presence and if it is in line with what they have presented on paper.

Think: Ready—Willing—Able

Ready, willing, and able are the guiding qualities of the candidate selection process. Looking first at the "able" category, your careful review of the résumés and applications will indicate if the required abilities are present. This is the easiest part of the process, since a candidate either has them or doesn't.

The next step is verification, which is a bit more complicated because applicants sometimes exaggerate their skills and duties on résumés, and you have to check that the facts are as stated. You know what applicants say they are able to do, but you have to be sure the words are truly matched by the deeds. You must verify what you think you learned about a candidate from the written document, and that comes during the interview.

Conducting the Interview

As with formulating the position description, conducting a successful interview involves planning and practice. You will probably spend twenty to fifty minutes with an applicant, and you must know how to gain the insight you need. To prepare, review the earlier chapter on the art of asking questions, and then write down the key questions you will ask at the interviews you conduct.

Verifying Abilities

The right questions will flesh out the applicant's abilities and produce examples that demonstrate those abilities. Matching your questions to the precise set of skills that the position requires will keep the interview from straying off target.

Keep questions geared to the requirements you articulated, and don't be satisfied with superficial comments. To get at the information you need, you have to probe deeply without coming across as an interrogator. Incorporate the questioning skills you've learned, and remember to take advantage of all of the appropriate techniques, including open questions, closed questions, probes, echoes, and follow-up questions. When you ask for and receive detailed examples of stated accomplishments, you will be more comfortable with your final hiring decision.

From Able to Willing

The interview will also help you determine if the applicant is willing to fulfill the responsibilities of the job. Unlike the tangible abilities, these are intangible personal qualities and are a little more difficult to pin down. How willing is the applicant to take charge, study, and learn new skills? Is the person flexible? Is the person a self-starter? Will he or she share information? Can he or she accept correction and direction? Will the applicant go the extra mile, help co-workers, take responsibility, and show initiative?

The answers to these questions are often gleaned from more pointed questions about the applicant's job experience. This is a time in which the active listening skills you developed in Chapter 8 will come in handy. You will be able to read and interpret clues that indicate if the candidate possesses the intangible willing skills that make for a good hire. For example, the candidate's description of skills learned in a previous job can disclose how little or how much the person grew in his or her previous position. If the candidate asks about training programs and schedules for training, this suggests a desire to continue to learn and lack of contentment with a rote job. From an applicant's description of committee work, you can deduce that the person is a team player and cooperates with fellow employees.

Always seek out evidence and documentation of these intangibles in action. Don't simply accept a generality such as "I welcome challenges." Uncover incidents that support the statement. One way of doing this is to ask candidates to tell you about a challenge they undertook and describe how they handled it. Apply the appropriate questioning techniques, and anytime you hear a generalization or an abstraction, probe for concrete examples. This way, you keep achievements at the forefront and won't get caught up in vagaries. You are going to hire the best candidate to perform a certain function, not just the best talker.

With this dynamic, in addition to answering your questions, prospective employees have a chance to stand out and to tell their complete stories when they might otherwise have been too nervous to summon up details. They will see that your interest is in their performance and that you want to know about them. This demonstrates to interviewees that you value them as people and as prospective employees.

From Willing to Ready

You can determine if an applicant is ready for the position at hand by identifying past patterns and using them to deduce the next stage in the person's professional development. By using the suggested questioning and listening techniques, you can learn much about the whole person, including personality and personal qualifications. You will want to take into consideration whether or not a candidate seems to have grown in past jobs. Has the person taken on ever-increasing responsibilities? Does the person display sufficient maturity to relate to a diverse group of co-workers?

Ultimately, you have to determine if the applicant will fit well with the departmental culture you've worked so hard to create. That doesn't mean that the individual has to be exactly like everyone else on your team, but all new hires should be compatible with those already in place. Benchmark candidates against the qualities you consider valuable to your department.

Targeting Scenarios to Generate Dialogue

Here are sample questions you might pose that will help to uncover how ready, willing, and able an applicant is:

- If you could have the ideal job at this time in your life, what would that job be, and what are the qualities that make that job ideal? Why do you feel you are qualified for it? In what ways have you exhibited the skills and traits that make you qualified for this job?

- Think of the best manager you ever had. What qualities made this person the best manager in your eyes? Do you possess any of these qualities? If so, when and how did you use those qualities? What are some of the qualities that the manager possessed that you wish you had or would like to improve upon?

- Think of the worst manager you ever had. What qualities made this person the worst manager in your eyes? Which of those qualities do you possess? Have you ever demonstrated those qualities? If so, what was the circumstance?

These questions are designed to initiate conversation and reveal elements of the candidate's personality. You could also describe a problem that you encountered in your department and ask applicants how they would handle it. Be sure to develop a dialogue; don't simply invite applicants to deliver a long speech, since they might be unsure of what kind of information you want. Don't ask applicants to envision a scenario that is so general and open-ended that they don't even know where to begin. Applicants are typically so nervous that this kind of conversational obfuscation could leave them disconcerted and leave you without answers.

Every Step Counts

To put you on solid footing before you must set out on an employee search, this final section recaps the important elements of the hiring process. First, be sure you know the exact skills required for the position. If you're thorough in your evaluation of the necessary skills and traits, you will be able to quickly conclude if candidates are likely to possess these skills, both from their résumés and during the interviews. If you don't know exactly what you want, you won't know if the candidate has it. Request the input and perspective of employees who hold or have held a similar position. Various points of view will assist you in developing a targeted job description.

When screening and interviewing prospective employees, concentrate on the ready, willing, and able items. Settling in to an easy and engaging conversation could distract you from your mission, which is to glean information pertinent to the candidate's ability to do the job and to do it well. Review the chapters on listening and asking questions before you hold interviews. By taking time and care to prepare, you avoid the high costs of a bad hire and the revolving door of employees.

Discovery Lesson 2

In your manager's journal, brainstorm other thought-provoking questions or conversations that will help reveal how ready, willing, and able an applicant is.

Questions to Consider

- *What are the actual skills needed to perform each of the jobs in my department?*

- *Who can help me get a clear understanding of what is really needed by people in my department?*

- *If and when I have to hire someone new for the department, how can I find applicants? Where can I interview them? How can I evaluate and compare candidates?*

There are two questions that rattle the human skull: How do you hang on to someone who won't stay? And how do you get rid of someone who won't go?

13

Conducting Meaningful Performance Reviews

PERFORMANCE REVIEWS ARE ESSENTIAL FOR developing your employees. They are also valuable to you. When the reviews are done correctly, your employees will learn how they are doing, what they should be doing differently, what their strengths are, what their weaknesses are, how they can improve, and what they need to reach their full potential. You, in turn, learn how to help them progress. To deliver valuable reviews, you need to invest in them, plan them, and schedule them.

Unfortunately, some managers are reluctant to conduct these reviews because the conversations are so personal, and if they are not done well, they can lead to hurt feelings or morale problems. However, when you approach your staff's performance reviews with an attitude of "I am investing in my employees," it will help you overlook the drudgery of documentation or the fear of staff members' reactions to the process. So, take reviews seriously and make them beneficial to everyone.

The Importance of Performance Reviews

As a manager, one of your primary responsibilities is monitoring progress within your department. Are you meeting quotas? Is production on schedule? Has inventory been consistent? When you measure these business metrics accurately and effectively, you can take action to correct where necessary, modify where appropriate, or reinforce where beneficial. Your employees are as important as any other asset in your business. Therefore, you need to monitor and nurture them as such. But they have an extra dimension; they are people with feelings and egos, and they depend on you.

They entrust you to provide guidance and direction to them, not only in their current role but also in their career. Therefore, to help them, you to need to track their performance and constructively communicate your findings to them.

Conducting a beneficial performance review begins with a plan. You must be clear about what you want to track and how you are going to track it, and you must confirm that your results, observations, and conclusions are correct. The best way to yield an accurate performance review is to make it a process, not an event.

The Performance Review Process

If you do your job correctly, there will be sufficient ongoing communication, so all your employees know what is expected of them and how well or poorly they are doing. That way, when the formal review date arrives and the discussions begin, there will be no surprises.

That's the way it should be, but not every manager lives up to this standard. In the following anecdote, the manager, Mike, thought he was doing well; he thought he was delegating, but his method and his intervention didn't lead to a productive outcome.

Mike said to his employee, Jake, after he was hired, "I describe my style of management as the Vacuum Theory of Management." When Jake asked what that was, Mike said, "As long as everything is going well, you won't hear from me, but the minute something goes wrong, I'll be all over you like a tent."

If Jake knew that before he accepted the position, his decision might have been different. Perhaps he didn't ask the right questions during his interview; if he had, he might have realized this approach would not be conducive to his professional development.

As it was, every time Mike came into Jake's office or even walked toward him, Jake's first thought was, "What have I done wrong?"

Mike thought silence was delegation and support. Unfortunately, that silence caused everyone else to wonder, "Am I doing OK? I haven't heard from him lately."

Preparing for the formal performance review with Mike was like getting ready to testify before a congressional committee. The event was tense because the manager was clearly in control and obviously liked it that way. The review was a report card on past activities; he was the teacher, and every employee was his student. Those reviews simply didn't work and were not effective two-way communications.

Though Jake was an able producer, and both he and the organization had made a substantial investment of time in his training, he soon resigned. Eventually, many others in the department were as disgruntled as Jake was by the Vacuum Theory of Management, and they too left.

Mike continued to hire new people, evaluate them, and eventually watch them leave. That cycle was both expensive and time-consuming, and it certainly didn't contribute to the long-term profitability of the company.

Recall from previous chapters the image of the master gardener tending a garden. Note the word *tend*, which means "to take care of, to minister to, to watch over, to look after." The gardener pays attention to the garden all the time. This includes tilling the soil, watering it as appropriate, and fertilizing it regularly. It's more than just selecting and planting seeds and then looking in on them every once in a while, because gardening is a continuous nurturing process. Similarly, as manager of your department, you must be attentive to your employees—all the time, even if you must use communication technologies to accomplish this.

Another way to look at the process-versus-event concept and the need to be continually alert is to compare it to driving a car. At the wheel, you are constantly observing traffic, pedestrians, and signs; measuring your location, your relation to other objects, and your speed; and making adjustments as necessary—slowing down, speeding up, changing lanes. You also watch the gauges to monitor fuel consumption, temperature, electrical power, pressure, and other indicators of how well or poorly your vehicle is running. You don't wait until the end of the trip to check these items to see how you did. That would incur the risk of not completing the trip. So, you check constantly to keep track of how you are doing. At the wheel of your department, you monitor similar indicators with regard to your employees.

Six Steps for Productive Performance Reviews

Let's assume you and the members of your staff are engaged in ongoing communication. You are now conducting a formal annual performance review with one of your employees, and you want it to be productive. You and he had previously agreed on specific goals and expectations that you're now reviewing.

This section takes you through the appropriate steps.

1. Identify what the employee has done well and what he has done poorly during the past year by citing specific positive and negative behaviors.

   The key word here is *specific*, because when you establish the area of discussion, you set the focus. When you concentrate on specific actions, both you and your employee will be discussing the same thing.

   For example, if tardiness is identified as a problem, a specific comment might be, "In the past two weeks, you have arrived at least 40 minutes late on six occasions." There is no question about those details. Now consider this opening sentence: "You've been coming in late a lot recently." Definitions are needed here to deduce how late is late, what constitutes a lot, and when is recently.

   When you begin the review, be sure that you and your employee are looking at the situation in the same way. Don't use vague words because they will only lead to vague discussions, and vague discussions usually lead to misunderstandings.

Be equally specific in commenting on positive actions, which should also be included in the review. A frequently heard comment in the workplace and elsewhere is "Good job." What does that mean? No one knows for sure because it's such a vague statement. Consider how much more of an impact the following statement makes because it is more precise: "You reduced expenses by 12 percent over the last month. Well done."

Here are two simple rules for achieving a direct, productive conversation during a performance review:

- Because the actions of an employee led you to a particular conclusion, when you begin the discussion, focus on the actions rather than on your conclusions.
- Encourage dialogue, and then listen to the reactions and explanations. Give the employee the opportunity to describe things as he sees them, while you listen, and then respond appropriately.

2. Once you have established the specifics of the discussion and have described your observations, stop talking. The employee will likely have a reaction, so listen to it. He may agree, he may correct, or he may want to expand. All of these responses are good because they all keep the dialogue engaged. Your task here is to continue to move ahead in order to improve his performance.

In addition to searching for facts, watch and listen for signals that reflect emotions the employee might have. Is he shifting in his chair? Are his eyes darting around the room? Is he stumbling over his words? These signs will help you understand how the employee is reacting to your comments, and that understanding will contribute to a meaningful review. If you gain insight on how the employee feels, you'll be better able to understand him. Ask appropriate questions to keep the dialogue going. (Review the chapter on the art of asking questions.)

3. Discuss a strategy for helping the employee improve on any negative habits and balance it with the implications of not changing the negative behaviors. While you don't want to dwell on the negative, it is important that he understand the potential consequences.

Describe the consequences in detail. For example: "I'll have to put you on probation for two months" or "You won't be eligible for the transfer until you are on time on a regular basis." By being specific, you will not appear to be casting idle threats with unfair generalizations.

Also use appropriate positive comments: "You're due for a promotion within the next quarter," or "There is a raise coming effective your next pay period," or "You are on target for a bonus this year." This will give the employee the incentive to improve.

Conveying the truth, both positive and negative, and clearing the air will contribute to a better working relationship. Be sure, however, that this clarity is connected to future actions and improvements that will benefit the company and the employee's satisfaction and performance. This leads to the next step.

4. Link past accomplishments to whatever changes are needed. For example, if the person was good with inventory in a prior assignment, show him how those same detail skills could help

him make specific improvements that you are seeking in order processing. Make sure the employee knows how the strength or skill he has demonstrated relates to what is expected of him in the future. Then help him understand how to make the necessary changes.

5. Agree on an action plan. Together, develop a plan for changing unacceptable behaviors to acceptable ones and for continuing behaviors that are positive. As the two of you develop this plan, ask probing questions to engage the employee.

   This simple technique encourages the employee to take responsibility for planning the course of action required to reach his destination. It's a powerful tactic because people are more likely to follow through on their own ideas than on what they are told to do by someone else. To accomplish this, use the word *you* when phrasing your questions. For example:

   - "What can you do to _____ ?"
   - "What ideas do you have for _____ ?"
   - "What suggestions do you have to _____ ?"

   In contrast, if you impose the solution on the employee, you might garner his agreement at the moment, but there may be little or no follow-through, and a prime opportunity will have been lost. Your goal is to extract a long-term commitment from your employee to modify his behavior, not just to placate him temporarily.

6. Follow up. "Agree on when you will meet again and what specific behaviors, actions, and attitudes you will review. When there is a clear understanding of what's expected and a clear plan for achieving it, future measurements and evaluations are easier and employees will become more productive.

Everyone Wins

Adhering to the aforementioned six steps will make discussions of performance meaningful to your staff and to you. In fact, how well you conduct your reviews with your employees may be one of the skills on which you are evaluated during your own reviews. Thus, applying these steps can contribute to a positive report on your performance review while you are helping your employees improve. With this process, everyone wins.

Conducting an effective performance review is not only good business but also the right thing to do. Your employees deserve to know how you rate their progress, so praising as well as correcting is appropriate. The most important concept to remember is that worthwhile performance reviews are the results of ongoing assessments and corrections. There should be no surprises in the formal review. And it should be a pleasant learning and planning experience for both you and your employees.

Questions to Consider

- *What do I need to know about each employee before setting up the formal performance review?*

- *What can I do during performance reviews to measure our communication? Specifically, how can I tell if we are communicating effectively and working toward improvement together?*

- *What is my plan for ensuring I stay involved over time and allocate enough time to conduct productive performance reviews?*

Outstanding managers make their presence felt without being obvious about their influence.

Excellent managers increase the value of the people reporting to them.

14

Delegating Effectively and Empowering Employees to Take Risks

WHAT A GREAT OPPORTUNITY! YOU have a group of people whom you employ to get work done and be productive members of your team. The best way to do that is for you and them to understand and leverage their strengths in terms of the goals of the department and the company as a whole. Embrace the chance to motivate others and enable them to grow and excel in their jobs.

This chapter shows you how to encourage employees to take risks and how you can best delegate responsibilities. If you are adept at delegating, your employees will feel safe and will be receptive to taking on additional duties. This precept is at the very heart of being a manager. You can't do everything yourself, and you shouldn't try. Instead, you must motivate other people to do things and to do them well.

This is easily said but sometimes a feat to pull off. Employees may be overly accustomed to doing a specific job in a certain way; giving them a new task or a new format for accomplishing that task might require a change in methodology that is uncomfortable. When you assign a task, you aren't giving up responsibility for it but rather allowing another to carry out the task instead of doing it yourself. The trick is doing everything within your control to help them meet or exceed your expectations of the results. A large part of that lies in your ability to incent and support them as they change and take risks. Once you have set up their environment for success, your job is to observe, guide, and protect the risk takers.

Delegation in Action

Here's an instructive account of how, by delegating well, an authority figure allowed someone he valued and trusted to take a reasonable risk. Although that someone was his daughter, the principles he employed in this personal situation also apply to business.

Larry's 16-year-old daughter, Susan, had just passed her driver's test and received her license. Several weeks later, the family decided to take a short road trip to visit relatives in a neighboring state. Susan asked if she could plan the trip and, of course, do the driving. After Larry and his wife gave their permission, Susan went to work on her plan. She got out the maps, checked the possible routes, and finally settled on the best (fastest) option. Larry could have told her what it was, but this was her trip and her plan.

When the day of embarkation arrived, Susan slid behind the wheel, Larry's wife sat in the front passenger's seat, and Larry settled into the backseat with a newspaper. Susan started the car, and they were on their way.

Larry made a big show of reading the newspaper as though he weren't watching where they were going. In time, he noticed that Susan was going a bit too fast and was in the wrong lane to exit onto another road. It was obvious to him that she was going to miss the turnoff.

Larry had a dilemma. Should he tell her and prevent her making a mistake, or should he bite his tongue and let her commit the error? He had delegated planning the trip to her. If he were to jump in and correct her, he would be removing the delegation and communicating a message that she was incapable of executing her task. If, on the other hand, he remained quiet, she would miss the turn, and that would add to the length of the trip.

It was a test of his mettle for Larry to sit quietly and watch as Susan sailed past the exit. In about 15 minutes (it seemed hours to him) she announced, "Something is wrong."

"Oh?" said Larry. "What?"

She pulled over to the side of the road, stopped, and unfolded the map. "I missed the turnoff," she said, "but we can turn around right up the road and get back to the exit in a flash." And that's what she did.

The lesson is clear. Larry let Susan take a reasonable risk. Sure, she made a mistake, but they ended up where they planned to go. It took a little longer, but that was of no real importance because Susan gained some knowledge that day.

Larry acknowledged afterward that his composure during the incident required courage. "Perhaps it also required a risk on my part," he said. "But I was just being a good father. I helped her to grow a little."

A main function of managers is to help their employees grow professionally. Encouraging them to take reasonable risks is a good way of performing that function.

Simply defined, a risk is any action that could result in adverse consequences. Fear of adverse consequences is the major deterrent to taking risks. It's a defensive reaction, which prevents people from moving forward. Obviously, it is in your best interest as a manager to reduce or even eliminate that fear among your employees. How you do that depends on the individual risks with which you're concerned.

Delegating Is About Reciprocal Trust

When you delegate an assignment or a project, you incur the risk that your nominee may lack the appropriate skills or knowledge to fulfill your expectations. For you to feel comfortable delegating to this person, you must minimize your risk by being sure the employee has the information, resources, and support necessary to carry out the designated task. That is, you must be convinced that you can trust the person to perform.

The employees you choose to put in charge of projects or assignments are also taking a risk. They're not sure how you'll react if they make mistakes. To reduce their fears, you must make it safe for them to take the risk of accepting your assignment.

Before this can happen, it's important that you convince yourself that effective delegation is good business. In your manager's journal, write down the benefits, both to you and to your employees, of delegating responsibilities to them. Be precise about what's in it for you and what's in it for your employees.

Minimize the Risks of Delegating

Making those lists in your manager's journal is excellent preparation, but you may still be hesitant about putting someone else in charge of a project. You may well feel that you can do it faster yourself, but that's not what managers do. Managers motivate other people to carry out the tasks while they supervise.

You can reduce your anxiety by satisfactorily answering three pairs of questions about the person you're considering:

- Does this person have the abilities to handle this project? How do I know?
- Does this person have the judgment to make the right decisions? How do I know?
- Does this person have the emotional maturity to overcome barriers that may be encountered along the way? How do I know?

How can you measure and answer questions about these variables objectively?

If you have been observing your employees regularly, you'll know when they are ready to step up to additional responsibilities. If you don't know, perhaps you should observe them a little more closely before you set up any new opportunity. It is always preferable to delay delegating and thereby increase the probability of success than to guess and be wrong. An error here could hurt both you and your employee, so don't act in haste.

If your answers to the three sets of questions are positive, you can be reasonably sure you will be delegating to the right person. Your next step is to minimize your employees' risk in assuming the responsibility you are about to delegate.

Minimize Your Employees' Risks

Once again, try to visit the situation from your employees' perspective by answering this question: Under what conditions would I be reluctant to accept a responsibility given to me by my manager? Write your response in your manager's journal.

For most people, the reluctance ultimately stems from fear, and fear can paralyze. Thus, you need to minimize fearful reactions in your employees to enable them to take risks.

Give employees permission to make mistakes by telling them to let you know if they need help, and don't reprimand them if they do. None of us performs perfectly or in the most efficient manner the first time we attempt anything new. Your employees are adults and deserve to be treated as such. Abusive language will provoke ill feelings, which will then restrict their willingness to risk anything.

Encourage them to take chances and to try bigger ones, and don't make them feel guilty if a chance they took didn't pay off. Start with smaller, more familiar tasks to ensure success. Being successful from the onset will give them more confidence to continue to try new, unfamiliar activities. If employees err in the assignment, help them understand what went wrong, and then give them another task or project. Even a failure is a valuable experience, since it shows the employee what not to do the next time. In short, don't penalize employees for taking risks.

Recall how you responded when you were a child and one of your parents asked you if you did something that you knew was a no-no, and you were guilty. Whether or not you told the truth probably depended on how your parent had reacted to you previously under similar circumstances. If you had previously told the truth and were severely chastised for your actions, you learned that the truth can hurt. On the other hand, if they appreciated the truth even though they disapproved of the action, and they told you so, you learned that telling the truth is the right thing to do.

Be a good authority figure to your employees by extending both guidance and support while you give them direction and latitude.

Delegate Effectively

Help your employees think through options, and encourage them to trust themselves. To delegate effectively, you must first realize that you're not just doling out work to employees and telling them to complete it. You're placing employees in charge of a project and giving them the responsibility for achieving an objective that you consider important. They need to understand and accept this premise before they can take on added responsibility. When you delegate, you share responsibility for outcomes. Help your employees understand the significance of their central roles and of your supporting role. You will help, and they will perform; you will coach, and they will complete.

Second, tell employees to whom you delegate what you want accomplished, and then invite them to decide how to do it. Although their way of proceeding may differ from your approach, the difference is irrelevant as long as they accomplish what you want in a timely manner. By allowing employees to come up with their own solutions or approaches, you're in effect saying, "It's your responsibility; you own it, and I trust you to do the quality job I know you are capable of performing."

If it's appropriate, ask the employee to create a plan for doing the project. Developing a plan often helps people clarify their purpose and even identify potential trouble spots before they start. That will further tip the balance toward success. The more the employee knows in advance, the better the performance will be.

Finally, establish follow-up checkpoints. In these meetings, you ascertain how the project is progressing, discuss any aspects of the assignment that may be confusing or need adjustment, and provide whatever other aid the employee may need from you. Your attitude when setting up these checkpoints should be that, as a manager, you have a vested interest in the success of the project, and the employee should view you as a consultant who is there to help him or her succeed.

One word of caution: Do not fall into the trap of micromanaging projects. Don't be like the parent who says to a child, "I trust you to cross the street by yourself, but just to be sure you're doing it right, let me hold your hand." Your employees do not need handholding once you've put them in charge of a project. What they need is your trust and the knowledge that you are available to assist when necessary.

Coach Employees to Excel

A student we know who was a top player on his school's basketball team suddenly stopped taking long shots or even short jump shots. He began limiting himself to the low-risk layup shots. After several such games, a confused observer asked him why he was taking only sure shots. He said, "Wouldn't you do the same if every time you missed a shot, the coach yelled at you? I just became afraid of taking chances. The price of taking a shot and risking missing it was just too great."

By not making it safe for this excellent athlete to take risks, the coach inadvertently discouraged him from playing his best game. You can avoid making the mistake this coach did by adopting these guidelines:

- Encourage your staff members to take reasonable risks; and encourage them to prepare for them appropriately. Help them learn to reduce their risk of "failure."
- Invite your employees to communicate openly. These communications include:

- Stating opinions
- Giving gifts of criticism to you and fellow employees
- Asking thoughtful questions
- Offering recommendations
- Make sure your invitations for comments are sincere. Don't tarnish them by making employees feel sorry they opened their mouths. Don't reject any criticism without first giving it ample thought.
- Thank them for their contributions. Use the listening and questioning techniques from previous chapters to make this a true dialogue between you and your employees.
- Respond to requests and reasonable favors in a way that doesn't make employees regret having asked you.
- Do whatever you can to gain your employees' trust.

Please note that this chapter advocates taking *reasonable* risks. Remember Larry and his daughter? If the car had been heading for a cliff, he would have inserted himself into the situation immediately, because that would have been a risk with dire consequences. Intervention would have been necessary in that case, but it certainly wasn't necessary just because she was going to miss an exit.

Allow your employees to try new things, while being watchful for inappropriate risks. Encourage employees to work *with* you, not just for you, by sharing your perceptions of what has to be done and then letting them select a plan of action. Although you may know one way to accomplish the task, it may not be the only or best way.

Delegation itself is a simple process. Everyone involved must have the same goal—and it's up to you as the manager to articulate the goal so that everyone has it straight—set up checkpoints, and give employees the green light to pursue the assigned project. All of this requires open and positive dialogue, and that means talking, listening, and responding appropriately to others.

The Role of Exemplars

If employees feel as strongly about the department and the goal as you do, they will feel comfortable and will rise to the challenge you set. You cultivate that feeling through your own performance. You must delegate because you can't do it all. Let others assume responsibilities they can handle, and give them the space to figure out how to fulfill them. Of course, they won't do everything right all of the time, but neither would you. When you and they join forces, you'll build a bond of trust and respect within the department. When someone makes a mistake, you should acknowledge it, but you don't have to support it. Your employees can learn to live with a flub, but they need the encouragement and freedom to seek better solutions, and they will if you model that behavior for them.

Use the example of your own best manager as your model of how to delegate and engender risk taking. Think about what impressed you the most in working for this person, and record your conclusions in your journal to remind you as time goes by. It's most likely your best manager practiced the principles advocated in this chapter. Learn from the people you rate as the best, and you just might avoid some of the trial and error that led them to their designation as successful managers.

This new behavior on your part is going to require practice. The accompanying two-part Discovery Lesson will help you understand the behavior changes needed for you to become comfortable with the approach and then put it to the test.

Managing is all about getting others to carry out responsibilities. Your application of the formulas and experiences covered in this chapter will aid you in accomplishing the dual obligation of effectively delegating work to others and providing your employees with an environment that allows them to realize their fullest potential. In this way, the working relationship between manager and employee is structured for the benefit of all parties.

Discovery Lesson

1. Complete the following sentence: "I would be more willing to take reasonable risks if my boss _____ ."

   Now answer this question: What do I have to do to make it safe for my employees to take reasonable risks?

2. The next time a departmental decision has to be made regarding an isolated task, ask for suggestions from your staff rather than dictating the solution. Choose a relatively safe subject, such as making a schedule, rotating department assignments, or setting up a display. Set the goals for the assignment, and then stand back to give employees room to respond. It may take a little time for them to assume that first risk, but once they start, they will continue.

   Provide guidance on how to implement the called-for action or resolve the conflict, and then support and enable the employees' decision as long as it addresses the goals you had in mind. Even if they decide on something different from your preference, endorse it if it accomplishes the objective. Problems typically allow for many different answers, and your staff just might sprout a great idea that wouldn't have occurred to you. When this happens, it reflects well on your employees and on you.

Questions to Consider

- *What are the benefits, both to me and to my employees, of delegating responsibilities?*

- *What can I do to show my employees that I want to protect them from hurting themselves? What kind of safety net can I spread?*

- *Why would my staff be reluctant to accept the responsibilities that I give them?*

- *Why would I be reluctant to accept responsibilities that my manager gives me?*

> *Effective meetings don't happen by accident; they happen by design.*

15

Mastering Productive Meetings Is as Easy as PIE

LOOSELY DEFINED, A MEETING IS an interpersonal vehicle for communication among individuals or groups of people for a purpose. It is an opportunity for a group of people to come together to share ideas. The extent of sharing runs the gamut from a "show and tell" by an individual to full and open dialogue by all in attendance. How do you decide which is right?

Don't automatically assume that assembling as a group is the most practical format for your purpose. If face-to-face contact isn't necessary, maybe a simple e-mail will serve instead. Today's workplace puts a wide variety of communication techniques at people's fingertips. To decide which to use for a given occasion, compare their relative merits. For instance, face-to-face interactions may be necessary to share materials and elicit immediate feedback. E-mail, conference calls, or Net meetings might be a better way to go if you need people's ideas but not their physical presence.

A questionnaire could be the most efficient and least threatening way of securing widespread participation, since people can respond from the relative safety of their offices or homes. Having determined what is required and what is available, use the technique that is justified by the task at hand. For our purposes, we will continue with planning the meeting.

Once you are sure you need a meeting and why that is the best option, it is important to answer these questions: "What is my purpose? Why is it important? What do I want to get out of it?"

People often say, "Let's have fewer meetings!" What they mean is, "Let's have fewer unproductive, wasteful meetings!" Amen! If you look at the reasons you thought meetings were a waste of yours and your colleagues' time, it was that the planners did not think them through or manage them respectfully.

Management is all about getting things done through other people. To be an effective manager, one of the most important things to master is effective communication with your staff. Therefore, meetings as a communication vehicle are essential to the survival of your department. Treat them as such when planning and conducting them.

We want to put you on the path to conducting more productive meetings. It is as easy as PIE! You just need to make them **Planned and Prepared, Interactive, and Efficient.**

To know whether you were well prepared, measure achievements against objectives; to know whether it was interactive, solicit feedback; to know whether it was efficient, review to see if you achieved your goals in the time scheduled or less.

The best way to do that is to ask four questions:

- How do I plan meetings?
- How do I prepare for them?
- How do I conduct them?
- How do I follow up?

Planning

Planning a meeting is something you are often in charge of, so it gives you a chance to model the behaviors, attitudes, clarity of purpose, and respect you want from your people. Meetings provide a tool for modeling the behaviors, professionalism, and culture you want to foster in your department. They are watching. Take advantage of it. What better way to teach than to show.

The first question you need to ask yourself before planning a meeting is, "Will a meeting solve a problem or reduce the time it takes to accomplish a goal?" If the answer is yes, then you are ready to plan your meeting. There are several more questions to consider when creating a meeting that is PIE.

1. What is the purpose of this meeting?
2. What preparation is needed?
3. Who will the attendees be?
4. What will the schedule and agenda be?
5. What will be the roles and responsibilities during the meeting?
6. Was it successful? How do you define/measure success?

It is in your best interest that your meeting preparation address these elements.

Clarity of Purpose

Make sure your purpose is clear when inviting people. Clarity of purpose drives the rest of your planning decisions. Consider the list below to determine why you are having this meeting. This may seem like a laborious, manual process, but once you get good at it, you will roll through it more naturally and quickly.

Effective, productive meetings have one or all of these three purposes. Meetings are used to:

- Inform, educate, or share
- Discuss, review, or clarify
- Connect or bring together a group for a specific reason or purpose

We interviewed one sales manager who had meetings every Monday at 11:00 A.M. He told us 15 people were due to attend; 10 of them were local, and 5 of them connected through a Net meeting. The only thing the attendees knew was that they had to be at the meeting by 11:00 A.M. and they had to e-mail their prior week's sales results to the participants by 9:00 A.M. Experience taught them that these were nothing but an administrative exercise. So they began to treat them as such.

Think about the deterioration in the culture, trust, and respect with each meeting and each e-mail. How much time will the attendees invest in getting prepared for the meeting? How attentive will they be?

However, even routine meetings can be valuable if they are handled correctly. If we just take the first step, you will feel how different the meeting can be. Let's take the same meeting and give it a stated purpose.

The purpose of this meeting is as follows:

1. To share successes and challenges experienced over the week so we can learn from each other for the benefit of all.
2. To help the sales teams review their results, recognize and reward successes, and prioritize challenges for each.
3. To reinforce a collaborative trusting environment where everyone knows his or her contribution will be reviewed and recognized.
4. To provide a consistent, controlled model for soliciting and receiving feedback.

What do I want to get out of it?
1. Keep my sales team engaged, driven, and connected.
2. Improve sales results over time

What if I communicated this to the attendees before the meeting? Think about the difference in the attitudes and the resulting trust and respect that would be built with each meeting and each e-mail. How much time would the attendees invest in getting prepared for the meeting knowing the purpose as stated above? How attentive will they be if they are encouraged to offer and receive feedback and share challenges? Feel the difference? The next key is thoughtful preparation.

Preparing

Preparation means doing all the necessary pieces beforehand to make the meeting as easy as "PIE."

Who Will Be Invited and Why?

Only people who are directly influenced by and related to the content should attend a meeting. The department should be covered at all times, and productivity continued. If the whole department is required to attend, you have to ask yourself who is minding the store. If only selected individuals are required to attend, decide who, as well as how they will be notified. In such cases, in the spirit of goodwill and information sharing, you may want to inform the other members of the department why they were not invited.

If there will be guests, who are they and what will their roles be? Will your staff be told in advance, and if so, how? Decide what method you will use to ensure that complete information is available to all parties.

For our example, as the manager, I might say, "I want all sales people to attend so they can share, learn from others, and make sure their activities and results are aligned with the team sales goals." This clearly states who I need at the meeting and why.

Scheduling: Time and Agenda

A successful manager conducts a meeting only because it is necessary and not because it is habit. Have you ever been to meetings you felt you did not need to attend? Or perhaps the meeting was valuable for the first 30 minutes, but not the last hour.

Too many managers have meetings for the wrong reasons, without enough preparations, and without the control needed to run them. When you and your employees are occupied at a meeting, the functional tasks for which you are responsible are not being performed. They will be taken care of sometime, of course, but they now have to be fit into the time remaining after the meeting rather than within the full workday. This is why short, concise, and productive meetings are so important. Everyone's time is valuable, so be sure you demonstrate your recognition of that value.

Assuming one of your goals is to minimize negative impact on productivity, choose a time and duration that is appropriate for the meeting. The meeting time is never perfect for anyone, so providing enough lead time before the meeting allows your employees to plan accordingly. As for planning the agenda, meetings that are too short have the potential of forsaking achieving objectives for brevity. On the other hand, studies show that people's attention spans have decreased as technology advances have increased. Meetings that run too long fall victim to that problem and the value for the purpose starts to decrease.

Parkinson's Law, named for C. Northcote Parkinson, a notable British economist, states: "Every job can be expanded to fill the amount of time allotted to it." If a one-hour period is scheduled for a meeting, the meeting will usually last an hour—or perhaps a little more. If it's two hours on the schedule, then that's how long the meeting will last. Choose your agenda with a finite purpose and appropriate schedule in mind.

Build an agenda carefully, and stay with it. Ask prospective attendees what issues they would like brought up so that you can include them as appropriate. If a suggestion doesn't fit the current agenda and is not urgent, put it on a future agenda. Allocate a time limit for each item to be covered, and plan how you'll keep track of the time from the very start of the meeting. If conditions require, you can always add time to a particular item by subtracting an equal amount from another item or by postponing the other item until the next meeting.

Print the agenda and distribute copies to all participants— prior to the meeting whenever possible but certainly no later than the start of the meeting. Have extra copies available for any unexpected attendees. If you delegate any part of this task to an employee, be sure the person understands the importance of a concise and readily available agenda.

Who Will Do What on the Agenda?

Designate the people who will be called on to give a presentation and what they will be expected to do. Since you want constructive input, you must enable the speakers to prepare by giving them sufficient advance information. Everyone expected to attend is entitled to have enough foundation and time to prepare and then contribute. By making your goals known sufficiently in advance, you will produce a more orderly and productive session.

Staff members should be able to suggest agenda items too, but this should be done well in advance of the meeting so that you are able to review the additions and make changes, if necessary. Surprise agenda items often contribute heat but little light to a meeting.

Final Preparation Tips Summary

- *Tip 1*: Set up multiple ways for remote participants to facilitate feedback and communication during and after the meeting. If people are not required, encouraged, or able to be an integral part of the meeting, they won't respect it. You need to remove any excuses for people not to respect the meeting.
- *Tip 2*: When possible, send the agenda and/or presentation materials to participants before the meeting with an expectation that they send feedback regarding them before the meeting. Invested participants are valuable participants.
- *Tip 3*: Store or save presentation materials in two places or formats, that is, in addition to whatever will be used for the meeting, in electronic or printed form. Have a backup copy somewhere with you. It can be electronically saved, sent through e-mail, or printed.
- *Tip 4* (specifically for remote access meetings): Do your best to ensure everyone has the materials, independent of any tech-

nology, that might be needed during the meeting. For example, if they cannot see the materials through the Net meeting, make sure they have their own copies of required materials.

Interactive

No matter how you choose to dispense information, allow and encourage participation as frequently as possible. Regularly seek out new and fresh ideas from your employees. When you have all the possible information available, you can avoid mistakes that might hinder your progress as a manager.

A recent survey of managers asked: What are the biggest mistakes managers make? As you read through this sampling of their responses, consider how you can avoid these errors in meetings you conduct. They cited these attributes of a poor manager:

- Assumes he or she knows what the problem is
- Assumes employees are as enthusiastic as he or she is
- Has all the answers
- Doesn't know what else is going on in employees' lives
- Frequently doesn't know what the real problems are
- Talks too much and frequently doesn't listen
- Doesn't seem to care what employees think or feel
- Doesn't encourage feedback
- Corrects more than praises

Have you or other managers you know ever made these mistakes? By avoiding these pitfalls, you will demonstrate to your employees how to conduct themselves in a meeting. Modeling professional behavior is much stronger and clearer than words.

Conducting Meetings

Though short and productive is exactly what both planners and participants strive for, most business meetings are just the opposite. The reasons for this are numerous. However, you increase your chances of success if you have prepared appropriately as described previously. The challenge now is conducting the meeting correctly.

To help guarantee the effort will be productive and informative, before the session gets under way, reiterate what you plan to accomplish. This enables everyone to get organized and helps keep the proceedings on target and on track. All members of the group will be better equipped to participate in both the discussions and the solutions, and that compounded strength will be a resource for you and them.

Throughout the meeting, use everyone's time well—it's expensive. Time is a nonrenewable commodity; when it's gone, it's gone. To use time well, you have to plan each meeting. You also have to sharpen your time-management skills. If you have planned and prepared well, you need only to make sure you stay on course. One secret to success during a meeting is making sure all interactions or discussions are tied to one of those goals. If they are not, cut them short. There is nothing more destructive in a meeting than allowing someone to rant on a tangent that is not applicable, positive, or productive. So, in the interest of problem solving, weed maintenance, and constructive criticism, stop them as respectfully as you can and move on.

Efficient

Efficiency is achieving your goals and objectives using a reasonable number of resources. How do you know you have been efficient? Listen and ask questions.

Conclusion and Follow-Up

Before you end, ask for a consensus on whether the specified objectives have been achieved. If they have not, identify what remains and when it can be completed. Think this one through. In some cases, you'll find that it makes sense to remand the unfinished business for discussions outside the particular group gathered. Be careful not to place unnecessary demands on others' time. A word of caution on the other side, though: be careful not to cut meetings short. If you do, people may leave with significantly different views of what happened and what the next steps are. Invest the time to ensure you achieved what was intended or more with the meeting before ending it. At the end of the meeting make sure you can answer these questions:

- Were your objectives achieved? How can you measure that?
- What are the action steps?
- Who owns them?
- When are they due?

These questions can be very beneficial in clearing up any important questions that might inhibit productive outcomes from your meeting.

Use the following Discovery Lessons to test some of the ideas in this chapter. To gain maximum benefit, put what you learn into practice so that these behaviors become a natural part of your management style.

In addition to identifying the missing pieces to the "PIE," techniques and skills of giving presentations are essential in professional development. Most managers concentrate on control, and they ignore how that control is packaged and delivered. How-

Discovery Lesson 1

Pretend you are responsible for preparing for and conducting the sales meeting described earlier. Note in your journal your schedule, agenda, and other preparations that would help you elicit a "PIE" meeting.

Discovery Lesson 2

A large food and drug retailer found that their management meetings were considered unproductive and expensive. They were not sure why, but here was how they used to do it.

The company's upper management hosted a meeting every Monday at 1:00 P.M. The meetings were conducted over the company's dedicated VPN (virtual private network), which incidentally slowed down Internet activity for anyone not in the meeting. Stores in remote locations across the United States were required to connect as well. Upper management would work through every agenda item, which, at times, took in excess of two hours to complete. To complicate matters, the people in the corporate office talked at, not with, the site managers.

They described products, promotions, and procedures that headquarters determined were most important. The managers sat in their offices at each location and listened to these descriptions and edicts. At the end of the meetings, participants were invited to send in questions if they had them. Participating managers described these meetings as "boring, expensive, and disrespectful." Given what you know about effective meeting management, describe the pieces that were missing from this "PIE."

ever, audiences and employees respond to the packaging and the delivery more than they do to the control.

If you have not already done so, do yourself and your employees a favor and sign yourself up for a presentation techniques class. You'll be impressed by how useful those tools are. Regardless of the delivery medium, the basic principles are essentially the same for every meeting you run. Simply put: plan, then execute.

The department meeting is an opportunity for you and your staff to join together to examine and resolve issues to the benefit of all concerned. So:

- Plan your meetings—in writing.
- Strive for the broadest participation possible.
- Make sure everyone agrees that your objectives were met.

Discovery Lesson 3

Next time you attend a meeting as a participant, note what was good about the meeting and what was not. Did you observe a particular technique or action that you could implement to advantage in your own meetings?

This change in perspective can pay dividends in your efforts to plan and execute the meetings that are your responsibility. For most of us, it is easier to see the shortcomings in what others do than in what we do ourselves. If you pay close attention to how others are running meetings, you'll accrue a wide range of ideas about what works and what doesn't.

The principles in this chapter are almost universal, although certain variations may apply to your organization or industry. Keep looking for ways to improve on your meetings and internal communications. These observations will lead you to insights and behavior changes that will profit your department and, ultimately, your company. Remember to always be a student, and keep learning.

Questions to Consider

- *Why do I hold meetings in the first place?*

- *Whom do I expect and/or require to attend? What is their function at the meetings, and what do they have to contribute?*

- *How can I best use meeting time? To discuss reports? To ask questions?*

Truth springs from argument amongst friends.

Don't be afraid of opposition. Remember, a kite rises against, not with, the wind.

When your emotions take control, your brain becomes disengaged.

16

Resolving Conflicts

THE PREVIOUS CHAPTERS INTRODUCED THE principles, tools, and skills for building strong interpersonal relationships and creating a healthy departmental environment. This environment is referred to as a problem-solving culture. Some of the building blocks of a problem-solving culture come from understanding and effectively resolving conflicts. So, what is a conflict?

What's a Conflict, Really?

Conflicts are crossroads. They can be internal or external, and, while we will touch on internal conflicts, much of this chapter will discuss external or interpersonal conflicts. Conflicts can also be positive or negative, so let your attitude be your guide.

An interpersonal conflict spawns from a difference in understanding, expectations, perspective, or approach. In addition, differences are inevitable because we are all unique. Our uniqueness results from having different experiences and "baggage." As a result, we often view the same environment and the same experiences differently. As a product of our history, we confront problems differently and have different opinions, values, and needs. The differences multiply when working in teams with multiple generations, diverse ethnic cultures, and a broad continuum of technology expertise.

Those differences alone do not necessarily cause conflicts. What causes conflicts is how we respond to and act out our differences. Generally, a difference becomes a conflict when it grows emotions, becomes subjective, and gets personal. For example, conflicts often start with comments such as "You're wrong and I'm right," "You can't do it that way," and "I'm in charge, so we'll do it my way." These are not productive. The attitudes these statements reflect make resolution difficult, if not impossible.

In contrast, you can enable parties to resolve a conflict if, as they see the signs of a conflict arise, you direct them to adopt and agree to the following attitudes:

- We genuinely want to resolve our conflict.
- We agree to separate the problem from the person.
- We're not in conflict; we are aligned in some way.
- We will work this through to an understanding or agreed-on acceptance.

These attitudes suggest that conflicts are opportunities for people to learn and either understand or accept the other's needs, desires, perceptions, and goals. And for the benefit of your team, they are opportunities to transform conflicting parties into collaborative parties who can work together and clarify their respective and mutual goals.

Three Examples of Conflicts

Review the following common workplace situations and suggestions. At the end of the chapter, determine your corresponding responses under "Questions to Consider."

Example 1: Performance Rating

A month ago, you assigned Josh, one of your staff members, a project, which he enthusiastically accepted. After completing it, he submitted a written report of what he did and his results. Now you are going to meet with him to discuss the report and your evaluation of his performance.

Josh believes he did an excellent job. You, however, rate the work he did, as well as his report, as only fair. You and Josh have a conflict in perception. How do you handle it?

Before you answer, consider these questions:

What did you do to ensure your expectations about what was needed were understood and measureable?

What specifically do you want to accomplish or achieve with the discussion?

How do your answers change how you might approach your discussion with Josh?

Other things to consider:

What if Josh is a remote employee?

What if Josh has a history of low self-esteem?

What if Josh is politically connected? That is, is a family
member of a higher manager?

What if Josh was historically considered a high performer?

What if Josh is in a "protected" class?

How do these questions change your thinking, evaluation, and approach to Josh?

Example 2: Group Consensus

A workgroup including four employees and a team leader develops an operational effectiveness evaluation form for your department. The final version has been reviewed and accepted by all five group members. When they present the form at the next meeting, 10 staff members approve it, but four do not. These are the reactions of the four dissenters:

Chuck: "I don't like it."

Marvin: "We don't need it."

Millie: "It's too short."

Jane: "It's not specific enough."

You are among the group of 10 who approved. You are now expected to help resolve the individual conflicts with Chuck, Marvin, Millie, and Jane and then present the consensus at an interdepartmental management meeting. Where do you start?

Before you answer, consider these questions with the intent to understand and address their real issues and reflect on what insights you gain. "Why don't you like it?" "Why don't we need it?" (Hint: You can ask why until you get something concrete. Don't respond until you do, or you will be perpetuating the conflict.)

Example 3: Meeting Expectations

Fred, the sales manager of a medium-size computer software company, has three salespeople working for him. About six months ago, the three employees requested a meeting with Fred to discuss their mutual goals and expectations. At the end of the two-hour meeting, they all agreed on mutual expectations they deemed reasonable. All parties felt aligned. The salespeople knew what they wanted from Fred, and Fred knew what he wanted from the salespeople.

One of the goals was working together to improve customer service. Fred agreed to help resolve sensitive customer-related issues as they arose in real time. Within three months, the salespeople grew frustrated by Fred's repeated failure to honor his part of the agreement because they counted on it and communicated it to the customers. Fred's failure undermined his salespeople's efforts and proved costly to the company.

Angered by the situation, the salespeople scheduled a confrontation with Fred, their manager. You are one of the salespeople and must present your case to your manager. How do you do it? Before you answer, consider these questions:

- How do you best demonstrate the effects/results of the failed expectation?
- What were the mutual expectations on response time?

As best as you can keep these things in mind, stick to the facts, consider what you learned about Fred, and focus on understanding, not accusing. Interpersonal conflicts can be useful if you and your employees approach them as opportunities to learn and grow.

Internal conflicts can be beneficial as well. We will review three of them by example. Let's say you are a successful salesperson and you enjoy your job. Because of your success, you are offered a position as sales manager. You face what is called an approach-approach conflict. That is, you want to continue to sell, but you also want the promotion. Confronting this choice, you have to thoroughly examine what's best for you and why.

A second example depicts what is called an approach-avoidance conflict. Here, you've been offered a high-paying job as a consultant for a company that sells computer software. The work is appealing to you, as is the money, but the job entails 50 percent out-of-town travel. That does not appeal to you, since you have a spouse and three children, and you don't want to be away from them for long stretches.

Finally, you may have an avoidance-avoidance conflict, which is characterized by the adage "caught between a rock and a hard place." For instance, you are offered a promotion that requires you to relocate, something you don't want to do for personal reasons. However, if you don't accept the promotion, you will have to remain in your current job, which you no longer find challenging.

In all three conflicts, as you weigh your choices, you learn about yourself. You learn what's important and unimportant to you, what you like and dislike, what you need to be happy with your life, what your values are and their relative strengths, and more.

Other Types of Conflicts

Conflicts come in all shapes and in various degrees of complexity. What follows are general descriptions of some familiar types. For each, think of actual examples from your own experience; note them in your journal under the appropriate headings: performance rating, group consensus, and meeting expectations. As you reflect on them, try breaking them apart to notice three things: (1) the actual difference, (2) the approach to the difference, and

(3) the resulting conflict. When you dissect them, you will start to see patterns.

- Two people have the same objective but can't agree on a procedure for achieving it. What they want to accomplish is the same; how they want to accomplish it is different.
- Two people consider their respective views or positions on a critical issue threatening to each other. Each believes that relenting will undermine his or her image.
- Two people's goals are not only different but also mutually exclusive. If we do A, we can't do B, and vice versa.
- Two people have different beliefs of what is right and proper concerning a sensitive employee matter.
- Two people who don't like each other have to work together on a project. Their only possible course of action is to find a way of completing the project to the best of their abilities.
- Your evaluation of what one of your employees contributes to the department is different from the employee's own evaluation.
- A person tries to impose his or her opinion or values on another person.
- The needs of two people working together are not being met to the satisfaction of either.

Strategies for Resolving Conflicts

Whether you are mediating a conflict between co-workers or are directly involved in a conflict with an employee or with a manager from another department, the following approaches can serve you well when applied judiciously.

- **Ask appropriate questions.** Let's use the reaction of Marvin at the meeting in the preceding group consensus example. Marvin says, "We don't need it." The following questions would help resolve the conflict:

  "When you say 'it,' Marvin, what specifically are you referring to? That form or any tool for evaluating effectiveness? Why?" Listen closely. Continue to ask calm, confident, clarifying questions to help you understand why he answered as he did. This approach to questioning helps you understand the reason for the conflict and how to avoid it in the future. You can use it whenever someone uses generalizations or abstractions.

- **Confront the conflicting party.** Confrontations should not be viewed as anything more than positive attempts to settle problems. They are necessary means for resolving differences. Let's say April expects June to fulfill a promise that June made to provide a mailing list. Several days go by and the list is not forwarded.

  It would be appropriate for April to confront June with a statement such as, "I did not receive the list you promised to mail yesterday. I'm sure it was an oversight, but when do you think I can have it? It's important that I get it as soon as possible." As you can see, this is a confrontation, but there is nothing combative about the overture.

- **Pose your dissonance.** Frequently, conflicts arise when a person's actions are not in harmony with his or her words. If you experienced such disharmony with a vendor, for example, you could pose your dissonance to your representative by restating your expectation compared to the vendor's actions. "I'm confused. You said that you value me as a customer, but when I come to you with a problem, I am not given the respect I believe

I deserve. Would you please 'unconfuse' me?" In this way, you force that person to take responsibility for resolving your problem.

Another tack might be, "If what you're saying is true, then please help me understand why my last two phone calls were not returned?" Facts can be useful in bringing antagonists closer to concurrence.

- **Be flexible.** In the interest of ensuring conflicting parties achieve their mutual objectives, both will have to give a little— but not grudgingly. Giving is not the same as giving up. When you give, it's a voluntary gesture of goodwill, whereas giving up is an admission of weakness or failure. Giving up is usually done with resentment, while giving reflects a caring attitude. You can demonstrate this by taking small, nonthreatening steps, agreeable to both parties, that will lead to a desirable outcome.

- **Define the components of a conflict.** A frequently voiced complaint between conflicting parties is, "I can't work with that person because we have a personality conflict." This comment is meaningless until the specific objection is made clear. What does it mean when two people have a "personality conflict"? What are the components of that conflict? Only when the conflict is defined in terms of what the parties need that they're not getting from each other can they settle it.

- **Focus on mutual objectives, not on personalities.** To move in a productive direction, answer this question: What specifically do we need when we get to the other side of this conflict? More than likely, it is not to abuse the other person. Stick to understanding and resolving the difference without making it personal.

- **If possible, compose a written agreement concerning the resolution.** Having a written agreement often prompts people to take their promises more seriously than they would otherwise. This is important in today's fast-paced, potentially remote environment, because it creates a reference that can be reviewed should the same conflict keep coming up.

The ideal goal of a conflict resolution is to achieve agreements that benefit both parties and strengthen the relationship of the conflicting parties. You will contribute to the well-being of your department if you teach your employees how to constructively and productively work through their conflicts with one another.

Questions to Consider

- *How would you resolve the conflict in perception between you and Josh in Example 1 in this chapter?*

- *How would you resolve the conflicts with Chuck, Marvin, Millie, and Jane individually and as a group in Example 2? How can your resolution help avoid conflicts in the future?*

- *What is your initial statement to the sales manager in Example 3? How would you end your meeting?*

- *Describe a recent conflict that you experienced. If you resolved it successfully, how did you do it? If you didn't, what did you do that you shouldn't have? If you had to do it over, what would you do differently?*

> *Don't try to reason with emotions, for they are unreasonable.*

17

Handling Harassment

HARASSMENT IS JUST PLAIN WRONG; there is never a valid reason or a good excuse for it. There is no way to justify harassment in any situation at any time with any person. During the course of your career as a manager, odds are you'll encounter a situation that qualifies as harassment. It seems that businesses face an ever-increasing number of harassment lawsuits every day. While this book does not address specific legalities or policies and procedures that are typically unique to each company, this chapter offers guiding principles for recognizing and dealing with harassment in its many forms.

Defining Harassment

A chief difficulty in dealing with harassment is simply developing an all-encompassing definition of the act. The predicament is similar to the ongoing debate among lawmakers regarding pornography. One of the more memorable quotes to come out of those debates is, "I can't define it, but I know it when I see it." Harassment, likewise, is an elusive presence that keeps the courts full and human resources departments busy. Dictionary definitions of the term include phrases such as "to trouble by repeated attacks"; "to continually disturb"; and "to torment, pester, badger, or vex." These definitions suggest that harassers victimize their targets by repeatedly violating their privacy and invading their space. This may include invasion in their virtual space through e-mails and messages or their physical personal space. Even when they're asked or told not to do whatever they're doing, harassers disregard such requests.

Everyone is entitled to privacy and space without having to justify it or earn it. As a manager, you must assure everyone in your department that you will not tolerate harassment. To back up this assurance, you must handle the problem if it arises. You do this by first being aware of it and then acting appropriately. Let's begin by looking at two examples.

Example 1: Off-Color Jokes

One of your employees, Jana, has made it clear to fellow staff members that she is offended by off-color jokes. Joel, another person in your department, gets a kick out of telling or sending such jokes. He seems to gain particular pleasure from seeking out Jana to recite his newest gag. Although she has pleaded with him to stop, he continues to ignore her request. In fact, the more offended she becomes, the more he does it.

Example 2: Unwelcome Contact

Melvin and Harriet are co-workers in your department. Although Harriet persists in joining Melvin at the lunch table every day,

Melvin has made it a point to ignore her and to seek other company. This has been going on for about two weeks. Recently, Harriet called Melvin at home several times just "to make small talk." Melvin has told her that he doesn't appreciate those calls and finds them disturbing. He also told her that he would appreciate it if she would find other people to sit with at lunch. All of these requests have fallen on deaf ears. Harriet even told him that he's being "overly sensitive" and mean.

Actions such as those of Joel and Harriet would qualify as harassment. Both examples reflect the harassers' major motivation, which is to gratify themselves at the expense of others.

A simplified way to look at harassment is as selfish behavior by a person who places more value on his or her desires and interests than on another's right to privacy. Such people consider their own feelings to be more important than those of someone else. Harassment can relate to sex, race, age, religion, size, physical ability, hair color, nationality, education, or a host of other characteristics, but the common denominator is that it is an invasion of an individual's privacy and space and a disregard for a person's desires.

Guidelines for Managers

To ensure zero tolerance of harassment in your department, you have a three-part mandate: be alert, take action, and don't encourage offensive behavior through silence.

Be Alert

At all times, observe what is going on in your department. Don't just look at conditions; be sure you see them. There is a big difference between the two. Looking is passive; it just happens. Seeing is active, and it entails your full attention and participa-

tion. Be alert to how staff members interact. Is there an attitude of cooperation, or is there conflict? If there is conflict, is
it directed toward someone because of a perceived difference
between that person and others in the group? Is there an "in"
group and an "out" group? If so, what determines the "in" and
the "out"? Does the "in" group torment members of the "out"
group?

If you become aware of anyone's privacy being invaded in any
way, be prepared to do something immediately. The sooner you
take action, the less arduous the correction will be. Remember, it's
a lot easier to extinguish a campfire than a forest fire.

Take Action

Performance reviews, which are the subject of Chapter 13, certainly would be an opportunity to address harassment by an
employee, but don't wait until the next scheduled review to take
action. Do it right away. The dialogue between you and your staff
member must be immediate as well as constructive, and it should
support as well as correct. Think of the performance review as
a process, not an event, which means that the observations and
conversations should be going on all the time.

When you identify what you think is inappropriate behavior,
acknowledge it right away to the person responsible; do it privately, and be specific. Specificity is essential because generalities
will create hostility and offer little or no chance to correct the situation. State clearly to the offender what was said or done, when,
where, to whom, and who else was present. In doing so, you frame
and direct the conversation, and you and your employee will be
talking about specific actions rather than general interpretations.

When your employee responds to specifics, there can be a suc-
cinct discussion that leads to a clear conclusion, but if you allow

the discussion to revolve around generalities, only confusion and resentment will result. The situation can then worsen, and you'll have an even bigger problem.

If it is required by your company policy, report the harassment to your supervisor. If a pattern of such behavior develops with an employee over time, this documentation will be important. There are a number of ways technology can be used to monitor, regulate, restrict, and protect privacy if necessary.

Don't Encourage Harassment by Remaining Silent

Part of your job is to promote and protect the welfare of all your employees. If you ever allow, enable, or encourage harassment by remaining silent, there can be at least two serious consequences. One, the situation can get out of hand quickly and become much worse, and two, you may be the one accused of harassment because you let it happen. Both of these consequences can have serious repercussions for you and your company.

There are at least three ways you may be alerted to a harassment situation. An employee may complain to you about another employee; you may witness or overhear behaviors that might be considered harassment; and you may see or hear about behavior that you are certain constitutes harassment.

If an employee complains to you about the behavior of another employee, the first thing you must do is listen carefully. Do not offer an opinion, and do not display emotion. Don't react rashly; at this point, all you have is the word of someone who has a vested interest in the charge. There may also be cultural sensitivities you may not be aware of as well. Instead, approach the situation by gathering data. Ask specific questions of the person complaining, and then ask specific questions of the person about whom the complaint was made. This is not the time for evaluating the answers but for collecting the information. Inform your supervisor of the situation and then conduct or cooperate in any subsequent investigation that may take place.

If you observe what may be harassment, ask the employee who was the target of the potential harasser if the behavior was indeed offensive to him or her. If the answer is no, no further action is required on your part. If the answer is yes, explain that such behavior need not be tolerated. Conduct an investigation to determine additional facts. Since you thought the behavior might have been offensive, you would be well advised to inform the employee responsible that there might be risks associated with the observed behavior. Do this in a friendly and matter-of-fact manner, not one that would seem to be corrective and accusatory, because the offending employee might not have been aware of the potential reaction to the behavior. An appropriate comment from you at this point could prevent an unpleasant situation in the future. Also, if it involves the Internet, don't make assumptions about employees' Internet activities. Verify.

When you see or hear a behavior that you are certain is harassment, it is your responsibility to stop it right away. Your acknowledgment of the situation and confrontation of the offender may be enough to end the behavior, but you may have to initiate appropriate corrective action to prevent it from happening again. This may include reassigning the offender to another department or shift or, eventually, termination. In any event, you should immediately report the encounter to your supervisor.

Keep a Tight Ship

Regardless of the form it takes, harassment is always about failing to respect others. To recognize these behaviors, be attentive to all that goes on around you that might interfere with the privacy of your employees or affront their sensitivities. Collect documentation about accusations of harassment, but don't judge quickly. Keep your management apprised, and if you observe harassment in any form, stop it right away. When your position on harassment is clear to all of your employees, their actions will reflect your model, and that will lead to a safe and productive work environment for everyone.

The following Discovery Lesson will help you practice the skills covered in this chapter and identify these kinds of situations. This all comes back to the differences between looking and seeing, because when you actively observe what is taking place around you, you'll be more likely to see problems developing in time to take appropriate action.

Discovery Lesson

This lesson is an exercise in observation and awareness. It is a chance for you to set your antenna to detect something that might be there.

As you move throughout your department, look closely and listen carefully to everything that is taking place. As employees are carrying out their tasks, what else is happening that might impinge on their performance? Look for any indication of an "in" group and an "out" group, and see how members of the latter are treated. Observe what impact that status has on job performance and the climate of the workplace. If there is tension, productivity suffers; if there is mutual support, that spirit of cooperation makes tasks easier for everyone, and that's what you want.

Sometimes language indicates problems. If anyone is being derided, for example, even casually, that might point to future problems. If some

continued

employees are "just having some fun" at the expense of others, that's a strong signal of growing difficulties.

Be conscientious about ensuring that the workplace is comfortable for everyone. If you sense that something might be wrong, get into high gear and address the issue right away. While we hope you don't find any evidence of harassment, it's better to look and not find it than to be surprised later by something you overlooked.

Harassment can be insidious. Offenders might not think they are doing anything wrong, and victims might not feel free to complain. It's your responsibility to be aware of the activities and reactions of both parties. Remember that harassment is not defined by sex, race, age, or other narrow categories; it is about respect. Whether the frequency of harassment complaints has increased because employees are more aware of the behavior or because it has become more prevalent or more visible, you are expected to model proper behavior and to protect those working under your direction. If you are aware, attentive, and responsive, everyone benefits.

Questions to Consider

- *What are you doing to foster a workplace that is comfortable for all of your employees?*

- *Can you identify an "in" group and an "out" group among your employees? If so, what are you doing about it?*

- *Is anyone on your staff excluded from non-work-related social activities? If so, why? Is there anything you can do about it? Is there anything you should do about it?*

> *You gain confidence by consistently doing the right things in appropriate ways. Find time to do things for others, little things that clearly say, "I genuinely care about you."*

18

Moving Forward

MANAGERS MUST UNDERSTAND THEIR STAFF members, recognize their abilities, and guide them to perform to their maximum potential so they benefit the organization as well as themselves. This book set forth the basic principles, tools, and guidance you need to become a successful, professional manager. The rest is up to you.

You have broad and varied responsibilities within the work environment, but your influence goes far beyond the workplace. Always remember that your behavior affects the lives of other people in a profound way.

In whatever you do—hire, fire, promote, transfer, counsel, correct, support, coach, guide, or discipline—keep in mind what impact you may have on the lives of others. Your employees have bills to pay, plans to complete, trips to take, dreams to ponder. How you treat them at work influences all of these acts. Do your job—that's what you get paid for—but do it with sensitivity and humanity.

Being sensitive doesn't make you a weak manager who is easily influenced. On the contrary, sensitivity requires strength of character, which is needed on the many days when you must do what is unpopular. Your challenge is to do it in ways that are not personally hurtful and ideally even helpful. Even bad news can be delivered in a manner that is not harsh or vicious. A thorough explanation can often avert future problems.

Some managers enjoy seeing themselves as tough as nails, and in some companies, that behavior might be rewarded. However, the art of successful management is seen when you make tough decisions without a rough demeanor. Be thoughtful, not emotional. When you have to say no, think through your options for delivering the message and the impact it will have. Instead of a simple "No," will your employees hear "Absolutely not!" or a regretful "Unfortunately not"? You have dozens of ways to communicate the same information while sending vastly different messages. Take care to send the exact messages you intend, and anticipate the consequences of your messages. Managing excellence requires open and constant, ideally positive communication. Think about not only the substance of your communications but also how you package it. Where, when, and how you deliver information can be more significant than the words.

This book has repeatedly highlighted the stature of honor and respect. Everything you do as a manager you do with and through other people. You now are better equipped with skills, techniques, strategies, and plans that will help you effectively interact with a disparate collection of individuals. In addition, your job requires that you eye the hard realities of profits, schedules, regulations, distribution, production, and a host of other demands. All of these elements, from people to profits, have to be balanced. Every facet of work, from the moment you walk in to the moment you leave, has to be managed within the framework of the people involved in making your business or department run smoothly and profitably.

Being promoted to manager is exciting and rewarding, but it also imposes an awesome responsibility because of the influence and impact you have on the lives of many people. When you carry out the job with care, you will do it well.

Once again, congratulations on your promotion to manager, and good luck!

Appendix

WE HAVE PULLED KEY POINTS from the text for you to distribute to your staff.

Chapter Quotes

- Professionals exhibit quiet strength to make the difficult look easy.
- Small acts of human kindness done consistently characterize a mensch.
- Treat people as if they are the most important person to you at that moment.
- Sensitivity is as important to managing people as music is to dancing.
- A professional manager is an effective teacher, a sensitive counselor, and a master gardener.
- Knowledge is power. To increase your knowledge, welcome your employees' opinions, criticism, and questions.
- Managing is an ongoing process of developing mutually rewarding relationships with your employees.
- Positive attitudes lead to productive actions; negative attitudes lead to unproductive actions. Adopt and encourage positive attitudes.

- People may forget what you said; they may even forget what you did; but rarely, if ever, will they forget how you made them feel.
- An attitude is a state of mind and a predisposition to actions based on what you tell yourself.
- Attitudes precede actions; positive attitudes lead to productive actions; negative attitudes lead to unproductive actions. Adopt and encourage positive attitudes.
- People who have positive attitudes tend to look at the whole. Those with negative attitudes do not see the *W*—they focus on the hole. Put a *W* in your life.
- Remove all limiting beliefs and excuses for achieving success. If is to be, it's up to me.
- Every action or reaction communicates something. Determining what each "something" is provides the enlightenment to respond with clarity, care, and purpose.
- When you're asking questions, view yourself as the student of the person you're questioning.
- Criticism is a valuable gift. But, to be viewed as such, it must be properly wrapped and sensitively presented.
- It is kinder to be gently direct than to be cruelly silent.
- As a manager, you are only as good as the people under your influence. Hire the best and treat them well to reap the most benefits from your employees.
- There are two questions that rattle the human skull: How do you hang on to someone who won't stay? And how do you get rid of someone who won't go?
- Outstanding managers influence without being obvious.
- Excellent managers increase the value of the people reporting to them.
- Effective meetings don't happen by accident; they happen by design.

- Truth springs from argument amongst friends.
- Don't be afraid of opposition. Remember, a kite rises against, not with, the wind.
- When your emotions take control, your brain becomes disengaged.
- Don't try to reason with emotions, for they are unreasonable.
- You gain confidence by consistently doing the right things in appropriate ways.

Essentials for Managerial Excellence

- Be sensitive to people's feelings, and be kind to them.
- Take time to make people feel special.
- Listen to people's emotions as well as their words.
- View people's needs and wants as valid.
- Choose your battles wisely.
- Respect people's differences.
- Avoid being defensive and placing people on the defensive.
- Give people the benefit of the doubt.
- Resolve interpersonal problems as quickly as possible, preferably before parting for any significant time.
- In short, treat people the way you would like to be treated: as a valued friend.
- Finally, never take people for granted—never.

What I Get Paid to Do

- I get paid to create a collaborative environment in which all contributors are motivated to be the best they can be.
- I get paid to help everyone understand how we can work together to achieve our department's objectives.

- I get paid to ensure that we are all clear about our roles in upholding the ideals and standards that define our department.

The Three Elements of Attitudes

1. What you tell yourself
2. Your state of mind resulting from what you tell yourself
3. Actions that stem from what you tell yourself, combined with your state of mind

Diagnostic Problem-Solving Questions

When faced with a problem, ask:

1. What specifically do I want? Is it reasonable (i.e., attainable)?
2. Am I committed to resolving the problem methodically and conscientiously?
3. If negative thoughts or outside influences are sidetracking me, what specifically can I do to rid myself of those thoughts and influences?

Characteristics of a Departmental Weed

Weeds are attitudes, behaviors, and actions that are:

- Not aligned with your departmental objectives and problem-solving culture
- Nonproductive and prevent the betterment of your department
- Noncollaborative and promote "siloed thinking" within your workgroup

Being an Excellent Manager Begins with Being a Good Person—a Mensch

A mensch is a respectful and genuine person who is sensitive and appropriately responsive to others' feelings.

A mensch exhibits, embodies, and consistently adheres to and advocates the following principles, attitudes, and behaviors in dealings with people:

- Be a perpetual student and learn from everyone, regardless of education, age, position, or status.
- In your desire to understand people, ask appropriate questions, in an appropriate way, at an appropriate time, and in an appropriate place.
- Act responsibly and kindly toward yourself and others.
- Listen attentively to what people say, both verbally and non-verbally, and respond appropriately to their messages.
- Demonstrate a genuine regard for all people's feelings, and accept those feelings as being valid.
- Be sensitively forthright and honest with people, leaving little to the fate of imagination and confusion.
- Don't allow defensiveness to dictate actions; all actions should be guided by a desire to be helpful and cooperative.
- Make people feel valued by asking for their opinions, requesting their help, praising commendable performance, and being polite and courteous at all times.

In short, by being considerate, righteous, and positive in dealing with people, a mensch builds healthy communication bridges.

Index

About the Authors

J. Robert Parkinson, Ph.D., was a member of the faculty of Northwestern University in Evanston, Illinois, and a consultant and trainer specializing in effective communication for major corporations, professional associations, and government agencies. The author of six books, he has served as the on-air host of numerous radio and television programs. He also writes a weekly newspaper column on business communication.

Parkinson provides a wide variety of professional services to organizations and individuals across the United States. He conducts seminars and personal coaching and counseling sessions in relationship building, management practices, and communication techniques. His professional activities have included extensive travel throughout the country as well as Europe, South America, Africa, and Australia. With his wife, Eileen, he lives in Sarasota, Florida.

Gary Grossman is the founder and president of Venn Strategy Group Inc. Venn helps companies measure and manage the financial impact of dependent business units working independently (the silo effect). Grossman is an international consultant and trainer with expertise in using business intelligence and technology to build an integrated performance-management culture. His clients have included several well-known companies, including Coca-Cola, Epson, and Avery Dennison. Grossman received an MBA in Marketing/Finance from DePaul University's Charles H. Kellstadt Graduate School of Business. He lives in the north suburbs of Chicago with his wife and twin sons.

For further information about the authors' backgrounds and their respective services, please contact them at:

Gary Grossman—www.vennsg.com
J. Robert Parkinson—www.jrparkinson.com
www.managingothers.com